ideas number one
ideas number two
ideas number three
ideas number four

Four Complete Volumes of Ideas in One

Edited by Wayne Rice and Mike Yaconelli.
Previously published as four separate books.

Your Idea May Be Worth $100

It's worth at least $25 if we publish it in a future volume of **Ideas**. And it's worth $100 if it's chosen as the outstanding idea of the book it appears in.

It's not really a contest, though—just our way of saying thanks for sharing your creativity with us. If you have a good idea that worked well with your group, send it in. We'll look it over and decide whether or not we can include it in a future **Ideas** book. If we do, we'll send you at least 25 bucks!

In addition to that, the **Ideas** editor will select one especially creative idea from each new book as the outstanding idea of that particular book—and send a check for $100 to its contributor.

So don't let your good ideas go to waste. Write them down and send them to us, accompanied by this form. Expain your ideas completely (without getting ridiculous) and include illustrations, diagrams, photos, samples, or any other materials you think are helpful.

FILL OUT BELOW

Name_____

Address_____

City_____State___Zip_____

Phone (____)_____

I hereby submit the attached idea(s) to Youth Specialties for publication in **Ideas** and guarantee that, to my knowledge, the publication of these ideas by Youth Specialties does not violate any copyright belonging to another party. I understand that, if accepted for publication in **Ideas**, the idea(s) becomes the property of Youth Specialties. I also understand that I will receive payment for these ideas, the exact amount to be determined by Youth Specialties, payable upon acceptance.

Signature_____

Write or type your idea(s) (one idea per sheet) and attach it to this form or to a copy of this form. Include your name and address with each idea you send. Mail to **Ideas**, 1224 Greenfield Drive, El Cajon, CA 92021. Ideas submitted to Youth Specialties cannot be returned.

ISBN 0-910125-25-2 (Ideas Combo 1-4)

ISBN 0-910125-00-7 (Ideas Complete Library, Volumes 1-52)

©Copyright 1968, 1969, 1970, 1975, 1979 by Youth Specialties
1224 Greenfield Drive, El Cajon, Ca 92021
619/440-2333

The material in this book may be photocopied for local use in churches, youth groups, and other Christian education activities. Special permission is not necessary. However, the contents of this book may not be reproduced in any other form without written permission from the publisher.
All rights reserved.

Ideas in this book have been voluntarily submitted by individuals and groups who claim to have used them in one form or another with their youth groups. Before you use an idea, evaluate it for its suitability to your own groups, for any potential risks, for safety precautions that must be taken, and for advance preparation that may be required. Youth Specialties, Inc., is not responsible for, nor has it any control over, the use or misuse of any of the ideas published in this book.

CHAPTER ONE: CROWD BREAKERS 6

Alvin Awards	6	Longjohn Stuff	28
Apple Paring Race	6	Mad Libs	29
Autobiography	7	Marshmallow Drop	29
Art Class	8	Monster Make Up	30
Baby Picture Guess	8	Mouthwash Mystery	30
Backwards Quiz	8	Musical Hats	30
Balloon Pop	9	Musical Mother Goose	31
Bandaged Hand Announcement	9	Mummy	31
Blind Mate	10	Nobody Nose	32
Bucket Roulette	10	Noodle Whomp	32
Bucket Trick	10	Nose Art	32
Buzz Buzz Little Bee	10	Nose Balance	33
Candy Race	11	Nylon Race	33
Canned Laughter	12	Obstacle Course	33
Chair Roulette	12	Onion on a Stick	34
Chiki Chiki	12	Patch Sew	34
Choo Choo	13	People Bingo	34
Coffin Measure	13	Ping-Pong Flour Blow	35
Compatability Test	14	Ping-Pong Ball Race	35
Coordination Clap	14	Plate Hypnotism	36
Corn Shucking Race	15	Poker Chip Pushups	36
Crazy Foam Hairdos	15	Pop Bottle Pickup	37
Dime Trick	15	Popcorn Stuff	38
Donkey	16	Psychological Sit-Ups	38
Egg Drop	16	Psychological Story	39
Egg Toss	16	Question and Answer Game	40
Egg Walk	17	Quick Draw Contest	40
Elephant Pantomime	17	Revolving Story	40
Find the Face	17	Ride the Tub	41
First Kiss	17	Romeo	41
Fixed Charades	18	Rubber Band Relay	41
Fly Family	18	Russian Roulette for Chicken Hearts	42
Flypaper Pass	18	Shoe Stretch	42
Foot Painting	18	Shoe Tie	42
Foot Signing	19	Shoulder Pin	42
Foot Wrestling	19	Sit Down Game	43
Fortune Teller	19	Situation Game	43
Forty Inch Dash	20	Skydiving Lesson	44
Fowl Bowl	20	Soap Sculpture	44
Frogman	21	Spaghetti Hairdos	44
Funnel Trick	21	Speech Spasm	45
Girls' Weight Guessing Contest	21	Squirt Gun Duel	45
Gleem Scream	22	Standing Broad Grin	45
Glove Milking Contest	22	Submarine Ride	46
Grape Grab	22	Take Off What You Don't Need	46
Hobby Hoax	23	Taxation Without Representation	46
Hot Potato	23	Ten Toes on the Rocks	47
Human Christmas Tree	24	Thread the Needle	47
Human Scrabble	24	Tomato Test	48
If You Love Me	24	Toothpaste Catch	48
In a Jamb	24	Un-Banana	48
Junk Auction	25	W.C.	48
Key Word	25	Walk the Plank	49
Leadership Achievement Test	25	Water Balloon Shave	50
Leg Lift	26	Water Eggs	50
Lemon Eating Race	26	Weight Guessing Contest	50
Lemonade Eating Contest	27	Whistle and Burp	51
Letter from Camp	27	Who Hit Me	51
Let's Get Acquainted	27	William Tell	52
Lipstick Mash	28	Wrap the Duck	52

CHAPTER TWO: GAMES 54

American Eagle	54	Chariot Races	61
Amoeba	54	Chariot Race Relay	61
Anatomy Shuffle	54	Clumps	62
Art Charades	55	Comparison Scavenger Hunt	62
Balloon Basketball	56	Crossword People	63
Balloon Bust	56	Do It On Paper Shuffle	63
Bumper Box Relay	56	Driving the Pigs to Market	64
Balloon Pop Relay	57	Earth, Air, Fire, Water	64
Balloon Smash	57	Egg and Armpit Relay	64
Balloon Stomp	57	Egg and Spoon Relay	64
Balloon Sweep	58	Egg Roll	65
Barnyard	58	Eskinose	65
Birdie on the Perch	58	Excedrin Wamp	65
Bottle Fill Relay	59	Eye Spy	65
Broom Hockey	59	Fan the Balloon	66
Broom Twist Relay	60	Flamingo Football	66
Bucket Brigade	60	Football Relay	66
Buzz	60	Forehead Race	66
Capture the Flag	60	Freckle Clumps	67
Caterpillar Relay	61	Furniture Smash	67

Giant Jigsaw Puzzle	67
Giant Push Ball	67
Grapefruit Pass	68
Happy Birthday Race	68
Hide the Counselor	68
Hula Hoop Pack	69
Human Lawn Mowers	69
Human Wheelbarrow	69
Hunters and Hounds	70
In and Out Race	70
Indoor Scavenger Hunt	70
Indoor Skiing	71
Indoor Olympics	71
Inner-Tube Olympics	71
Inner-Tube Relay	72
Inner-Tube Soccer	72
John-John	72
Kill the Umpire	73
King of the Circle	73
King of the Goats	73
King of the Mountain	74
Kleenex Blow	74
Lemon Pass	74
Lifesaver Relay	74
Line Pull	75
Mad Ads	75
Matchbox Race	75
Mindreading Games	76
"Black Magic"	
"Book Magic"	
"Car"	
"The Nine Mags"	
"Red, White and Blue"	
Monocle Relay	77
My Ship Sails	78
Needle in the Haystack	78
No-Can-See Relay	78
Paper Airplane Derby	78
Pike's Peak	79
Pillow Case Race	79
Pin the Donkey on the Tail	79
Potato Race	80
Rhythm	80
Sack Race	80
Shoe Kick	81
Shoe Scramble	81
Shoe Shucking Race	82
Shoulder Shove	82
Snow Fight	82
Snow Sculpturing	83
Spoon Relay	83
Squatters Smash	83
Streets and Alleys	84
Stripper Relay	84
Symbol Rhythm	84
Thimble Relay	84
Three Legged Race	85
Tiny Tim Race	85
Toilet Paper Relay	85
Tug-O-War	85
Twister	85
Waddle Walk Relay	86
Waddle to the Bottle	86
Water Balloon Blitz	87
Water Balloon Relay	87
Water Balloon Shot Put	87
Water Balloon Toss	88
Water Carnival	88
Wells Fargo	88
Wheelbarrow Eat	89

CHAPTER THREE: THE HOT SEAT 90

CHAPTER FOUR: CREATIVE COMMUNICATION 98

Cop Out	98
Discussion	98
"Language"	
"Models"	
"Church"	
"Honesty"	
Groupers	100
The Island Affair	102
Will of God	104

CHAPTER FIVE: SPECIAL EVENTS 105

Bigger and Better Hunt	105
Blow Out	105
Come As You Were Party	106
Crazy Daze	107
Fight Night	108
Hogwash	109
Man Hunt	110
Mission Impossible	111
Old Timey Night	112
Peanuts Picnic	112
Poster Contest	115
Race Riot	115
Treasure Hunts	116
Wednesday Night at the Movies	120

CHAPTER SIX: SKITS 121

An Evening with Grandma	121
Crop Duster	123
Frontier Mortician	126
Herkimer the All-American	131
King and Queen Opera	133
Leaving Home	136
Little Red Riding Hood	136
Mad Reporter	138
Magic Bandana	139
Midget Skit	140
Mother, I'm Dying	141
Newlyweds	142
One-Liners (58 Short Skits)	143
Psychiatrist	153
Quickies (6 Short Skits)	155
Rinse the Blood Off My Toga	156
Skydiver	164
Spontaneous Melodrama	166
Stand In Skit	169
Tadpoles Skit	170
Ugliest Monster in the World	171
Wild West Show	171
You Got Me, Buddy	172

CHAPTER SEVEN: PUBLICITY AND PROMOTION 174

Action Handout	174
Contemporary Card Handouts (21 Handout Ideas)	175
Free Ticket	177
Peep Box	178
Mailers (11 Ideas)	179
Silk Screen Printing	186

For faster service call toll-free 800/776-8008

There are lots more ideas where these came from.

This book is only one of an entire library of **Ideas** volumes that are available from Youth Specialties. Each volume is completely different and contains dozens of tried and tested programming ideas submitted by the world's most creative youth workers. Order the others by using the form below.

Combo Books
All 52 volumes of **Ideas** have been updated and republished in four-volume combinations. For example, our combo book **Ideas 1–4** is actually four books in one—volumes 1 through 4. These combos are a bargain at $19.95 each.

The Entire Library
The **Ideas** library includes every volume. See the form below for the current price, or call the Youth Specialties Order Center at 800/776-8008.

IDEAS ORDER FORM

Combos ($19.95 each)
☐ Ideas 1–4
☐ Ideas 5–8
☐ Ideas 9–12
☐ Ideas 13–16
☐ Ideas 17–20
☐ Ideas 21–24

☐ Ideas 25–28
☐ Ideas 29–32
☐ Ideas 33–36
☐ Ideas 37–40
☐ Ideas 41–44
☐ Ideas 45–48
☐ Ideas 49–52

☐ **Entire Ideas Library—** 52 volumes and Index for only $199.95 (regularly $269)

☐ **My check or money order is enclosed.** (CA residents add 7.75% sales tax; SC residents add 5% sales tax.)

☐ **Bill me.** (Shipping charges plus a 5% billing charge will be added to the total.)

SHIPPING CHARGES	
ORDER SUBTOTAL	ADD
$ 1.00– 9.99	$3
$10.00–24.99	$4
$25.00–49.99	$6
$50.00–74.99	$7
$75.00–99.99	$9
$100.00 and up	$10

Name _____

Church or org. (if applicable) _____

Street Address _____

City _____ State _____ Zip _____

Daytime phone (_____) _____

Clip and mail to Youth Specialties, P.O. Box 4406, Spartanburg, SC 29305-4406
or call 800/776-8008
Prices subject to change.

Chapter One

Crowd Breakers

ALVIN AWARDS

This is a good gag to catch your audience off guard. Announce that Mr. and Mrs. J. P. Alvin (or any name, for that matter) have given a special trophy to be awarded to the outstanding young person of the year. Make a big deal on how the winner was chosen for their hard work, honesty, character, etc., and then announce the winner. (Audience will applaud.) The winner should be a girl. She comes forward, dressed nicely for the occasion, and you have on the table in the front of the room, a large trophy. (Borrowed from someone.) The girl steps up to the front and you say something like, "And now we would like to present the first annual J. P. Alvin Award . . ." You reach for the trophy, and instead, pick up a shaving cream or whipped cream pie that is sitting right behind the trophy, and not seen by the audience. You smack the girl right in the face with it. (She has been clued in ahead of time, and expects it.) While you are laughing, she gets a pie from under the table and hits you with it, and you hit her back with another, and so on. The girl's boyfriend can also get into the act, by protesting the pie, but he gets clobbered as well with a pie, then he starts throwing them, too. A "free-for-all" develops, and the slapstick type humor is really wild. As many people as you want can get involved, but you should be careful not to let it get out of control.

APPLE PARING RACE

Have several kids race to see who can peel the longest continuous strip of peel off of an apple with a paring knife. Give the winner a sack of apples or a bottle of cider.

AUTOBIOGRAPHY

This is a monologue, that is, a routine for one person. It should be memorized, not read. Timing in the delivery is important. A second way to use it which can be a lot of fun is as follows: Send four guys out of the room. Bring one of them back in and tell him that he is going to test his abilities as a stand up comedian. You will read the following script to him, and he must remember as much of it as he can and do it without the written script for the second guy who will be brought into the room at that time. The second guy then must do it for the third guy, and so on. By the time the fourth guy gets it, it will be only about one paragraph long and so bad that it will be hilarious.

The script:

I was born at an early age in a hospital, to be near my mother. We were so poor that we didn't live on the other side of the tracks. We lived in the middle. When I was young my folks moved a lot . . . but I always found them.

My mother and father are in the iron and steel business. My mother irons and my father steals. Our neighborhood was so bad that when they tore it down they built slums. I was a tough kid. In fact, I was the only kid on the block who had barbed wire around the top of his playpen. Tough? Why man, I was four before I knew I had fingers. And the neighborhood was tough too. Any kid with two ears was new. Any cat with a tail was a tourist. Our main fun time was playing stick ball in the street. When it rained I played right gutter. I was ugly too. When I was a baby my mother didn't push the baby buggy, she pulled it. I had long curls until I was ten. I wish you could have seen the look on the little boy's face the day I got my hair cut . . . the little boy that used to carry my books to school.

It was in high school that I had my first romance. My first girlfriend was different. She had very affectionate eyes . . . they looked at each other all the time. I won't say she was crosseyed but every time she cried the tears ran down her back. The doctor called it bacteria. And she had lovely golden hair down her back. None on her head . . . all down her back. And there was something strange about her teeth. She was the only girl I knew who on Halloween bobbed for applesauce. And she was fat! She sat in my English class . . . in the first two rows. But I didn't mind because anywhere I sat in the room I was next to her. The teacher didn't mind either because every time she turned around she erased the blackboard. Why, we were downtown one day and she got weighed on one of those scales that give your weight on a little card. Hers said "one at a time, please." One day she was wearing a red, white and blue dress and five people tried to mail a letter. And was she lazy. Every Saturday all she did was sit around the house . . . and she was so bowlegged that she sat around the house. I remember the first time we met. She was sitting on a bench near the cafeteria. I sat down beside her and she cocked an eye at me, I cocked an eye at her and there we sat looking cock-eyed at each other. The last I heard of her she had run off with another guy and got married by a Justice of the Peace. After the ceremony the guy asked the Justice of the Peace how much he owed. The Justice said, "Just give me what you think she's worth." So the guy gave him a quarter. The Justice gave him fifteen cents change.

ART CLASS

Explain that you are an artist in your spare time and that you are going to paint a "human painting" right before the audience's eye's. The scene will be in the forest, and you will use people instead of paint. Have someone come up and be the "babbling brook" by standing up front going "babble babble babble..." over and over. Next have someone come up and be the rustling trees. He stands next to the babbling brook and goes "rustle rustle rustle... etc." Do the same thing with the "whistling grass" and the "howling wind," and then ask for someone to come up and be the picture frame. The frame runs around the other guys who are babbling, rustling, whistling, howling, etc., and he continues to run around them. While they are all doing their part, you say, "And now, ladies and gentlemen, there you have it. The babbling brook, the rustling trees, the whistling grass, the howling wind, and the RUNNING SAP!"

BABY PICTURE GUESS

Obtain baby pictures of as many members of your group as possible. Slides are best. If you do get snapshots or portraits, however, shoot slides of them so that they can be projected with a slide projector. Each member of the group then is given a piece of paper and pencil and tries to guess who each baby is as the pictures are projected. Whoever gets the most correct answers is declared the winner.

BACKWARDS QUIZ

This one would work great with the "Hot Seat" (see page 90). While a kid is sitting on the seat, ask him simple yes or no questions. He must answer the question correctly, but shake his head incorrectly. In other words, you might ask him, "Are you a girl?" He must answer "No" while shaking his head "Yes." If he goofs it, he gets zapped. If you do not use the "Hot Seat," just ask several guys five questions each and see who does the best. Send them out of the room and bring them in one at a time so that they don't practice while watching the others.

BALLOON POP

Have several kids come to the front of the room. Each gets a balloon. They must blow up the balloon until it pops. The first to do so is the winner. The last to do so receives a penalty. For fun, give one person a larger balloon that takes forever to blow up, but don't let him see the others' balloons before the race.

BANDAGED HAND ANNOUNCEMENT

This is always great at camps or larger meetings. Simply walk to the front of the group with a serious look on your face and make the following announcement. Be as convincing as you possibly can.

> "I'm sorry to have to put a damper on the meeting, but I have a very important announcement to make. A few moments ago, one of the girls in our group went home. One of the guys here . . . and I won't mention his name . . . did a very crude and insensitive thing to her. While she was sitting on the bench outside, minding her own business, he approached her and very rudely tried to kiss her. He was trying to be smart, I suppose, but the girl reacted negatively and was deeply offended. When the guy tried it a second time, she swung at him with a pencil she had in her hand and seriously gashed his hand with it. The guy had to have his hand bandaged, and the girl left and probably will never come back to one of our meetings again. Things like this are needless and are a sign of immaturity. We cannot tolerate this kind of child's play anymore. I don't think I need to say anymore about it . . ."

Usually you can hear a pin drop when you are finished making the announcement. All the while, you keep your hand in your pocket. After the announcement, casually take your hand out of your pocket (in plain view of everyone) and reveal your hand, all bandaged up with blood stains all over it. As soon as the kids notice it, the laughs begin.

BLIND MATE

Select three couples to compete in this simple game. One at a time, each couple is blindfolded and then separated by a distance of 20 feet or so. The pair must then walk towards each other, locate the other person and hold hands. The couple to do it in the fastest time is the winner. To really make this tough, turn the players around a few times before they begin.

BUCKET ROULETTE

Select three volunteers. Show them several buckets (three is enough). Tell them that one contains water, the others only rice. One at a time, they choose a bucket and get the contents of it dumped on their heads. They can draw straws to see who goes first. If he is lucky, it will be only rice. The next person chooses from the buckets that are left. It is over when somebody gets the water. You may use as many people in this as you want, but usually three is enough.

BUCKET TRICK

This is one you play on the entire group. You need one helper. Announce that you have a bucket of water from the fountain of youth. (Or any story you want to make up.) Have a volunteer take a drink of the water (he is your clued-in helper). The bucket is brought in, and the audience cannot see inside it, but it is really a bucket of rice or confetti with a dipper sticking out of it. Inside the dipper is some water. The outside of the dipper must be dry so that no rice still stick to it. You take the dipper out of the bucket, pour the water into a glass, and the volunteer drinks it. He waits, starts acting like a two year old, grabs the bucket, and throws its contents all over the audience.

BUZZ, BUZZ, LITTLE BEE

Introduce this little game by explaining to the group that you are going to give a lesson on the facts of life, or "the birds and the bees." However, due to a lack of time, we only have time today to cover the "bees" part.

Next, select a volunteer from the group, who you know is a good sport and will play along with a degree of enthusiasm. Seat him in a chair at the front of the room, facing the group. Explain to him that he is to pretend that the room is a garden, and the stage area is the beehive, and that he is the queen bee, the ruler of the hive. You are the worker bee. You will go out into the garden and gather the pollen and bring it back to the hive. When you return to the beehive with your load of pollen, you will say (in bee language), "Whompf!" The queen bee (your volunteer) must say it back: "Whompf!" Have him practice it a few times, and when he does it good and loud, have the group applaud.

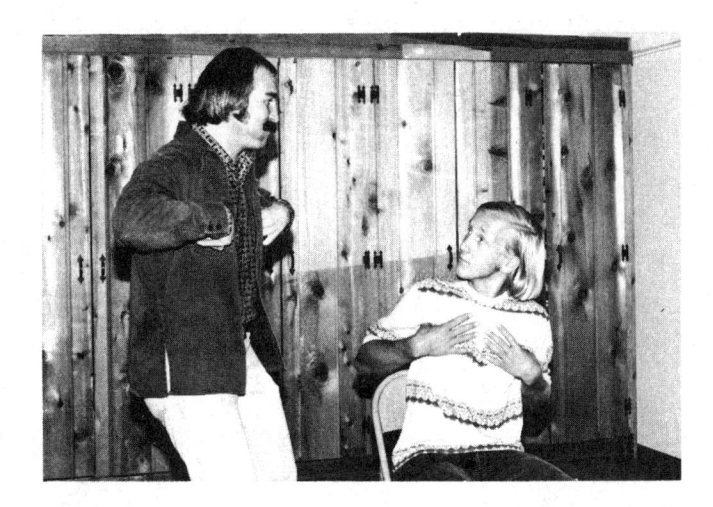

Then you will go out into the garden again and gather a second load of pollen. (When you go out into the group, you should use your arms like wings, buzz a lot, and make this a fun thing to watch.) When you return to the hive with your second load, you say, "Whompf! Whompf!" The queen bee must say it back: "Whompf! Whompf!"

The third time, you go back out into the garden for your third (and final) load of pollen. This time, when you return to the hive, you will have so much pollen that you can't even talk. Your little bee cheeks (your mouth) are so full, that all you can do is just stand there and buzz. This is the signal to the queen bee that he should say, "Buzz, Buzz, Little Bee. Give it all to me." Have him practice that phrase as well.

You go out for your third load of pollen, but when you do, you go behind a wall or chair, and get a mouthfull of water. You return, and as instructed, the queen bee says "Buzz, Buzz, Little Bee. Give it all to me." At that point you spit your mouthfull of water all over your queen bee.

Note: This stunt is as much a skit as it is a "trick" or "fall guy stunt." Sometimes it is wise to clue your volunteer in ahead of time and make sure that he doesn't go "Oh no you don't! I'm not going to get water spit all over me!" at the wrong time. It should appear that your volunteer has "fallen for it," and it can be done that way if you are able to choose a good sucker, but sometimes it is wise to "fix it."

CANDY RACE

Tie a piece of candy onto the middle of a length of string and have two kids on each end of the string with it held in their teeth. On a signal, they chew the string towards the candy, and the first to reach the candy and get it in their mouth wins. No hands are allowed.

CANNED LAUGHTER

Bring plenty of empty soft drink cans to the meeting and have three or more kids compete to see who can stack them the highest within a given time limit. The winner may be awarded a six-pack of his favorite pop.

CHAIR ROULETTE

This is simply musical chairs for big boys. Have 5 or 6 big guys walk around chairs (one less than the number of guys). Leader yells "stop!" and they grab a chair and sit down. Whoever is left without a chair is out. Remove one chair and do it again. Two guys finally fight over one chair. Winner gets a prize.

CHIKI-CHIKI

Four volunteers come to the front of the room and line up facing the audience. You are on one end of the line, and you are all standing side by side. The volunteers must do exactly what you do because it is a coordination test to see (1) how well they can follow the leader, and (2) how well they can improvise on what he does. The audience will be the judge as to who does the best job.

Begin by swinging your arm in a circular, sweeping motion, and reach over and pinch the volunteer standing next to you on the cheek and say "Cheeky Cheeky." Then that guy does the same to the next person in line, and so on. Next you wind up and grab the other cheek, and do the same. Then you pinch his nose in the same way, saying "nosey, nosey," and his chin while saying "chinnie, chinnie." With each of these, the same action is repeated down the line.

What makes this funny is that before your pinch the guy next to you each time, you put lipstick on your fingers with a tube that you have in your other hand, but concealed to the guy next to you. You just keep smearing lipstick all over the guy's face, the audience gets a lot of laughs, but the poor guy has no idea what they are laughing at.

Note: It is wise to instruct all the guys to stand with their hands behind their back. That way you can keep the lipstick tube behind your back.

CHOO-CHOO

Send a few people out of the room and bring them in one at a time for this stunt. You have a choo-choo train (made up of boys and girls holding onto each others waists and moving around the room going ch-ch-ch-ch-ch, etc.), and it is the first choo-choo to Hawaii. You bring in a guy, and ask him to be the caboose. He is instructed to just hang on and do what everybody else does. So the train goes around the room and the guy in front stops the train and says "Welcome to Hawaii" and puts a Hawaiian lei on the neck of the girl behind him, and gives her a kiss on the cheek. The girl says "Welcome to Hawaii" to the guy behind her, and gives the lei, and kisses the guy on the cheek, and so on, down to the final girl, who takes the lei, puts it around the neck of the last guy (who was brought in) Welcomes him to Hawaii, and then slaps him hard on the cheek. The look on his face is priceless, as he was also expecting a kiss.

COFFIN MEASURE

Have one boy volunteer to show the group how to be measured for a coffin. Put a blindfold on to give the feeling of being dead. Lay the boy on a table and begin measuring. Measure from head to shoulder, from shoulder to hand, from waist to foot. Then lift up his left leg and measure from his leg to hip. Lift his right leg and pour a cup of water down his pant leg.

COMPATIBILITY TEST

This crowdbreaker is designed after television's "Newlywed Game," only it is not necessary to use newlyweds. Simply select two or three couples that have been dating for awhile and have them come to the front. The guys leave the room while you ask the girls a few questions about their boyfriends, like "Is your boyfriend tight or generous when it comes to spending money on a date?" or "Is your boyfriend a good or bad driver?" The boys are then brought back into the room and must answer the same questions. If their answers are the same as the girls', then they receive points. If they are wrong, they get points taken off, or receive a penalty of some kind. One suggestion would be to have the guys answer the questions while sitting on the "Hot Seat" (see page 90). If he answers the question incorrectly, he gets zapped.

CO-ORDINATON CLAP

This is a crowd breaker that you can use anytime, as many times as you want. It is always fun, gets good laughs, and involves everyone. The procedure is very simple. You cross your hands in an up-and-down manner (vertical), and the group must clap every time your hands cross in the middle. If your hands stop and do not cross, then the audience must not clap. That is basically it. The fun is when you fake the group out by almost crossing your hands but stopping just before they do. Go fast, slow, and point out people who goof it up by giving them a penalty of some kind, such as the "hot seat." You may also keep it up and when anyone goofs, they are out of the game. Keep going until there is only one person left, and give him a prize.

CORN SHUCKING RACE

For this little game, you will need several ears of corn. Select three or more volunteers to try and "shuck" an ear of corn using only their bare feet. No hands are allowed. Whoever finishes first, or whoever has done the best job within a given time limit is the winner. Award an appropriate prize, such as a bag of corn chips.

CRAZY FOAM HAIRDOS

Select three couples for this event. The guys sit in chairs and their girl partners stand behind them. Each girl is given a can of "Crazy Foam" (available in most toy stores) and on a signal, must create a "hairdo" on top of her boy partner's head with the foam. She should first apply a lot of the foam on the boy's head, then with her hand, fashion it into some kind of style. The audience judges to determine the best job.

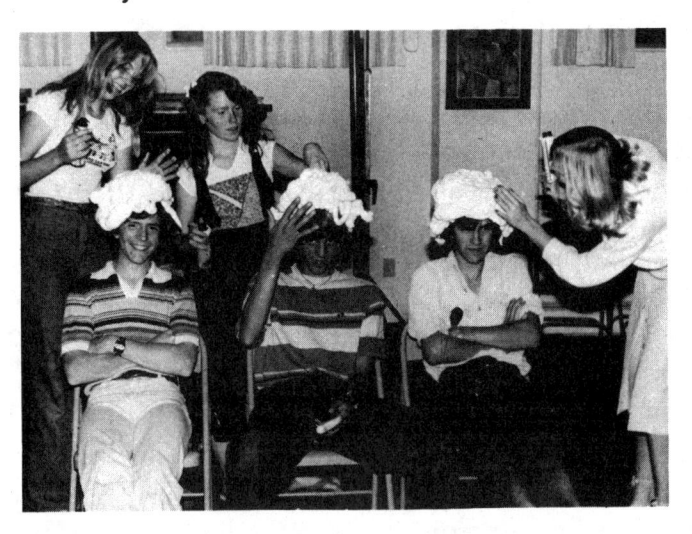

DIME TRICK

Take a dime, wet it and press it firmly against the forehead of a volunteer. Ask him to try and shake it off. The dime will stick with surprising strength, but he will be able to shake it off after a few tries. Try this with several volunteers, as a contest to see which player can shake it off in the fastest time. For fun, when you stick the dime on the last player's forehead, quickly take it off without him knowing it. It will feel like it is still there if you press firmly on his forehead. He will try to shake it off, but it just won't fall (because it's not there). You'll need to practice removing the dime ahead of time so that your volunteer doesn't suspect anything.

This can also be used as a kind of "fortune telling" gag. The number of times it takes for you to shake the dime off is the number of years that will pass before you get married, the number of kids you will have, the number of times you have been kissed, etc. Of course, the person with no dime on his forehead will have a very high number for his answer.

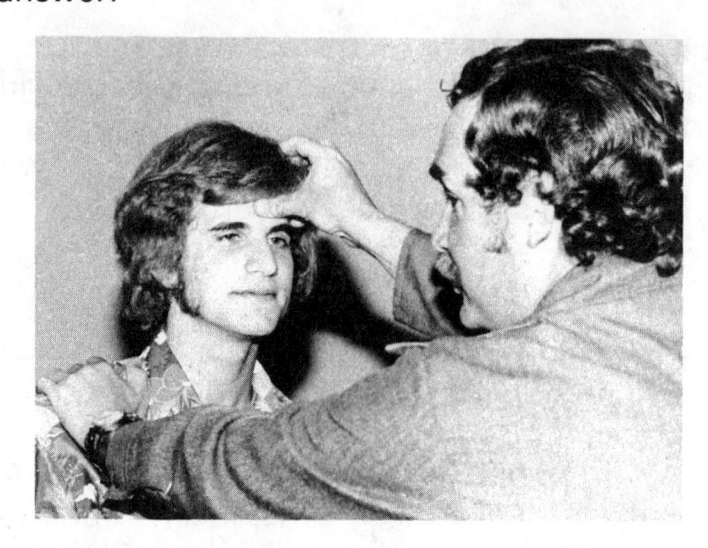

DONKEY

Have five or six volunteers come to the front of the room and announce to the group that each volunteer will be secretly told the name of a barnyard animal. When you count to three, each of these people will then try to make the sound of the animal that they were given as loudly as possible. The audience will judge to determine who has done the best job. The winner will get a nice prize.

Then you proceed to whisper the name of an animal (Cow, Duck, Pig, etc.) to each of the volunteers. However, instead of giving them an animal, you tell all but one of them to not make a sound. You tell the other person to make a sound like a "Donkey." Of course, he thinks that all the others have animals just like he does. Just before you count to three, remind them again to make their noise as loudly as they can. The result will be a slightly embarrassed "donkey." Don't forget to give him his prize.

EGG DROP

Select three couples to compete in this game. The boys lie down on the floor and the girls stand over their heads holding a raw egg chest high. The boys must keep their arms on the floor. On a signal, the girls drop the eggs on the boys' heads and the boys try to catch the eggs on the way down. Anyone that succeeds avoids having egg all over his face.

EGG TOSS

Three couples line up with the partners facing each other about three feet apart. Each couple is given an egg. They toss the egg back and forth, each time taking one step backward. Whichever couple can keep the egg from breaking the longest is the winner. Water Balloons can also be used instead of eggs.

EGG WALK

Lay eggs all over the floor and then blindfold a boy or girl and have them walk across the room without stepping on any. Substitute the eggs with peanuts after they are blindfolded. Put plenty of peanuts around and watch them scream.

ELEPHANT PANTOMIME

You pantomime that you are washing an elephant in front of the audience and in front of volunteer A. (Volunteers B and C are out of the room). Only the audience knows what you are doing. The volunteers do not. After A watches you do the pantomime, B is brought into the room and A must do the pantomime for B, even though A may not know exactly what he is doing. He just tries to duplicate what you did. Then C is brought in and B does the pantomime (as close as he can get it) for C. The result is a lot of laughs, because the pantomime keeps getting farther and farther away from the original. Let the volunteers try to guess then what they were supposed to be pantomiming.

The original pantomime that you do should include the following: Pull the elephant in on a rope. Tie the rope at a stake. Dip a rag in a pail and wash the side of the elephant, jumping high to get all the way to the top. Crawl underneath, wash his belly and legs. Go to the front and wash his trunk, inside and out, and wash the elephant's ears as well. Then wash under his tail, hold your nose, etc., and generally try to be as creative as possible.

FIND THE FACE

Before the meeting, shoot three or four photos of kids with a Polaroid camera making the most distorted, ugly face they can. The idea is to disguise yourself without using a disguise, but by looking as crazy as you can. Then, during the meeting, choose three or four other kids to come to the front. On a signal, each is given one of the photos and they try to identify the person in the photo by looking for them in the audience. The first to do so wins. This is best used in larger crowds, where everyone is not easily recognized or acquainted.

FIRST KISS

Three guys are sent out of the room and it is explained to the audience that when each guy comes back in, one at a time, no one is to talk or make any noise. The first word that the person says is the first word he said after he kissed his girlfriend for the first time.

FIXED CHARADES

Two volunteers are sent out of the room with an assistant who explains to them that they are going to play a simple game of "charades." They each get a movie, book, or song title that they must get the audience to identify. Whoever does it in the fastest time wins.

Meanwhile, you reveal to the audience (while the volunteers are out of the room) what the titles are that they will be "charad-ing." The first person will have a fairly difficult title like "Mutiny on the Bounty." The audience should guess it after about 10 seconds or so. The second person will have a ridiculously easy one like "Tea for Two." The audience should guess everything but the correct title. For example, if the person makes the letter "T" with his hands, the audience should guess "Time Out," or "Hand Signal" or anything but "Tea." The result is a very frustrated volunteer.

FLY FAMILY

Send 3 or 4 kids out of the room. When they return one at a time tell them they are going to be introduced to the "Fly Family." There are then 4 people who stand in line with their hands behind their backs who are the Fly Family: Mr. Horse Fly, Mrs. Horse Fly, Mr. Butterfly, and finally Mr. Letterfly. They are introduced one at a time shaking hands. Letterfly throws a cup of water all over the unsuspecting fall guy.

FLYPAPER PASS

Bring a toaster and a piece of bread to the meeting. You will also need to obtain a piece of flypaper (if you can find any). Anything similar to flypaper wll work, if flypaper is not available. It doesn't even have to be sticky, but that adds to the fun of the game. Kids simply pass the flypaper around the room when you push the bread down into the toaster. Whoever is holding the flypaper when the toast pops up must eat the toast with something foul tasting on it, such as sour cream, tabasco sauce, limburger cheese, etc.

FOOT PAINTING

Choose a group of boys (number of boys should be one-half the number of letters in the name of your group, church, organization, etc.). They all sit down in a line facing audience. You paint the letters in the name of your group on the bottom of their feet (jumbled up) with a felt marker or poster paint. At a signal, they are to try and get the letters unscrambled and in order (readable) without any of them getting up or moving from their positions.

FOOT SIGNING

Have five guys come to the front of the room and remove their shoes and socks. Give each a felt tipped or ball point pen. On a signal, the five boys run out into the crowd and see who can get the most signatures on the bottom of their feet in the time limit. No one person can sign more than three feet. Guys can use both feet. Signatures must be legible.

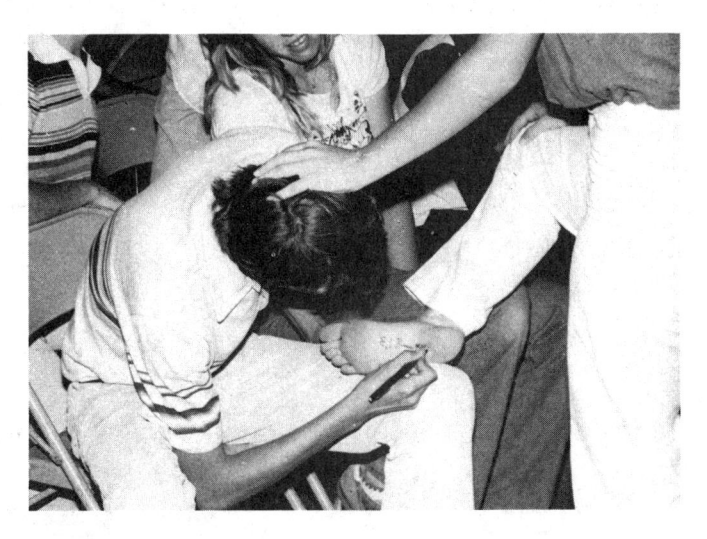

FOOT WRESTLING

This is just like Indian Arm wrestling, only you have guys sit on the floor, lock toes, and then at a given signal, try to pin the other guy's foot on the floor.

FORTUNE TELLER

Bring an adult "guest" to the meeting and announce that he has "supernatural" powers to tell the past, predict the future, and so on. He chooses two or three "subjects" (kids in the room) and pulls out bits of humorous (but true) information about them, much to the amazement of all. Of course, you have gathered this information ahead of time on the sly from the kids' parents. After you have had some fun with this, clue the audience in.

FORTY INCH DASH

Give three kids a 40 inch piece of string with a marshmallow tied to one end of it. On a signal, each person puts the loose end of the string in his mouth and, without using his hands, "eats" his way to the marshmallow. The first person to reach the marshmallow is the winner.

FOWL BLOW

Obtain about three to four feet of clear plastic tubing (surgical tubing) or hose, and by tapping two small holes in the opposite ends of an egg, you can insert the insides of the egg into the tubing. After you get the egg inside the tubing, have two guys who are real "blowhards" get on each end of the tubing, and at a given signal

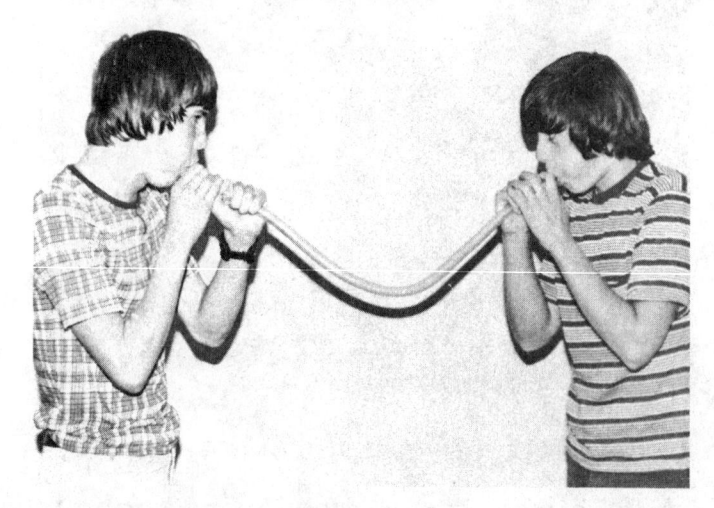

begin to blow on their end of the tubing. Object is to keep the egg away from your side, and blast the other guy with it.

FROGMAN

Choose two boy volunteers and give each a swim mask, swim fins, and a snorkel. They are instructed to leave your meeting wearing this gear and go up to houses in the neighborhood as a representative of the city sanitation department. Each boy must convince the person at each house to allow him to go skindiving in their bathtub. They can make up any story that they want, but a suggested one is that they are checking the water for pollution, since there have been reports that garbage has been leaking into the city's water lines. An assistant should go with each player to record the results and to make sure he doesn't cheat. You are not allowed to tell the people at each house that the whole thing is a gag. The time limit is 20 minutes. Score 1 point for every house that agrees to let you swim in the bathtub. Whoever has the highest score is the winner. When the guys return, let them share their experiences. (Incidentally, they don't have to swim in the tubs, only get permission. As soon as the person at the house agrees, then they can be told that it is a gag.)

FUNNEL TRICK

Place a funnel in a boys pants (in front). Have him tip his head back, then place a nickel on his forehead. The object is for him to drop the nickel into the funnel 3 times in succession. The third time pour a cup of water into the funnel while his head is tipped back.

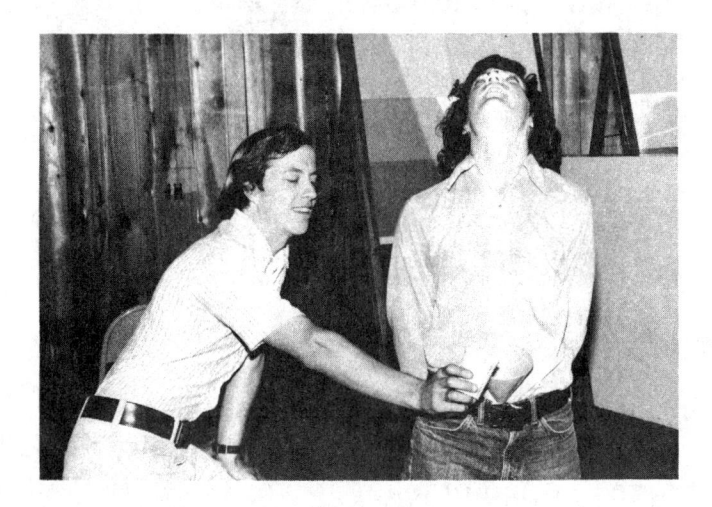

GIRLS WEIGHT GUESSING CONTEST

Have an assistant take three girls out of the room and weigh them. (It would be best if your assistant were a girl, and if you didn't choose girls that had obvious weight problems to be weighed.) Then bring the girls back in, and send out three guys who think they are pretty good at guessing weight. While they are out, announce the TOTAL weight of the three girls to the audience, and the guys must come in and guess the combined weight of the three girls. Let each guy examine the girls closely and make a guess by adding up the weight of each girl. Whoever comes the closest wins.

GLEEM SCREAM

Have two or three guys race to see who can brush their teeth and get them the cleanest within a given time limit. Give each guy a (new) toothbrush, a glass of water, and a tube of toothpaste. In one of the toothpaste tubes, however, you replace a bit of the toothpaste with something that tastes real bad. (Use limburger cheese, Brylcream, etc.) This can be done by dipping in the end of a toothpaste tube with a drinking straw and taking out some of the toothpaste, then you can replace it with something else.

GLOVE-MILKING CONTEST

Fill two rubber gloves with milk. Punch pin-holes in the ends of the fingers and hang them from a stick held over two buckets. Two guys then attempt to "milk" the gloves. Whoever gets the most milk into the bucket within the time limit wins.

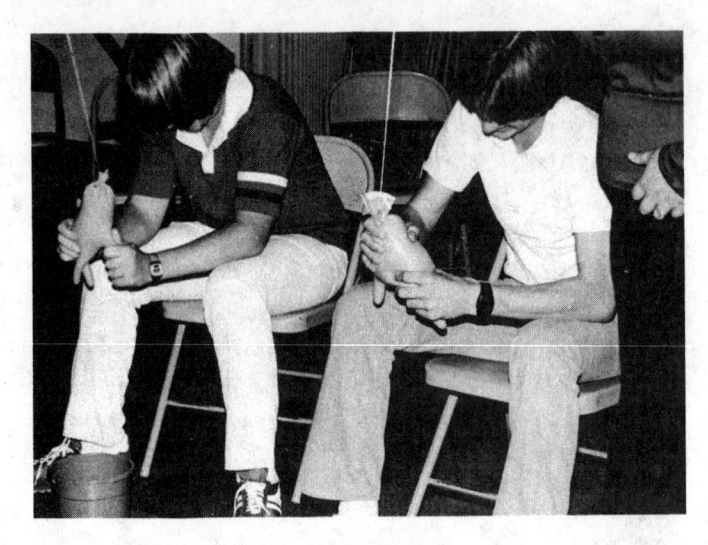

GRAPE GRAB

Prepare ahead of time two or three dishpans with solid jello in the bottom of the pans. Grapes are at the bottom of the jello. Then have three kids (one per pan of jello) attempt to retrieve the grapes from the jello and put them in a glass jar without using their hands. They must grab the grapes with their teeth. Whoever gets all their grapes in the jar first, or whoever gets the most in before time is up, is the winner.

HOBBY HOAX

Choose three guys in the room who have a hobby of some kind. (Any hobby) You explain to them that you are going to ask them questions about their hobby, and they are to answer, but not give away what their hobby actually is, because the audience is going to later guess what the hobbies of the three boys are. Then send them out of the room (supposedly so that the audience can think up some questions). While they are out, you tell the audience that they are to assume that all three boys' hobby is KISSING. (Regardless of what their hobbies actually are.) Call the boys back in, and ask them questions like the ones below. Their answers will be hilarious.

1. Who taught you your hobby?
2. How long does it take to do your hobby?
3. In which room do you perform your hobby or in what place?
4. What sound does your hobby make?
5. Is there any special training involved? If so, what?
6. How old were you when you first learned your hobby?
7. How do you get ready for your hobby?
8. What's the best time of the day to perform your hobby?
9. What do you wear when you are doing your hobby?
10. What sort of special equipment do you need?

HOT POTATO

The "Ohio Art" Toy Company manufactures a toy game called the "Hot Potato" (called "Spudsie") that is a great game for use as a crowd breaker. You wind it up and pass it around the group, and after 15 seconds or so, a bell rings inside the potato. Whoever is holding the potato at that time is the "loser" and receives a penalty of some kind, such as the "Hot Seat." When you pass it around, the following rules apply: (1) You cannot throw it, (2) You must take it if someone hands it to you, (3) If you drop it, it is still yours until you pick it up and get it going again, and (4) You may hand it back to the person who gives it to you if you choose.

HUMAN CHRISTMAS TREE

This is great idea for Christmas parties or meetings during the holiday season. Divide the group into teams and give each team plenty of Christmas tree decorations (lights, balls, tinsel, construction paper, etc.) Each team then selects one of its members to be decorated like a tree. Set a time limit (10 minutes maximum) and whichever team does the best and most creative job of decorating their "human Christmas tree" is the winner.

HUMAN SCRABBLE

Divide group into teams. Distribute at random cards which have a letter of the alphabet written on them. On a signal, each team must use the letters which they have and form the longest word that they possibly can. The longest word wins. Mix all the letter cards up again, re-distribute them and play several rounds. Each round has a thirty second time limit. Be sure and include plenty of common letters (especially vowels). For a variation of this game, see the game "Crossword People."

IF YOU LOVE ME

Choose someone in the room to be "it." They must go up to someone in the room and say, "If you love me, honey, smile." The person must reply, "I love you, honey, but I just can't smile," without smiling or they become "it." The person who is "it" may do anything (make faces, etc.) except touch the other person.

IN A JAMB

Challenge a guy that he cannot hold an egg with two fingers for 15 seconds without dropping it. When you get someone to accept the challenge, have him extend his two fingers through the space at the hinge of an open door (between the door and the door jamb) and place the egg between his two extended fingers. Count off the 15 seconds, and then just walk off and leave him there.

JUNK AUCTION

As a great fun activity and also a great money raiser for your group, collect a lot of interesting "junk" that you think kids might really go for, and auction it off. You'll be surprised at what kids will buy for unbelievable amounts of money. Be creative in your auctioneering, and make funny routines to "sell" your items to your crowd. This works best with a large group. When the bidding is good, the results are hilarious.

KEY WORD

At the beginning of your meeting, explain that there will be certain "key word." (Tell them what the key word is, such as "elephant," "stink," etc.) Explain that you might use that word in a sentence at any time during the meeting, and when they hear it they are to stand to their feet at once. Last person up gets a penalty.

LEADERSHIP ACHIEVEMENT TEST

Announce that you are giving a test to determine the leadership potential in the group. Those who are able to follow the directions on the test are the real leaders of the group. Tell them to work fast because the best will be timed and they only have three minutes to complete the test. Pass it out face down, then start everyone on the test at the same time.

LEADERSHIP ACHIEVEMENT TEST

Directions: Answer each question in sequence. If you do not know an answer, go on to the next one. Read through entire test before starting on question number one.

1. Print complete name in upper left hand corner.

2. Print address _____

3. Underline the correct answer:

   A. A good leader must be: Dogmatic, Restrictive, Dedicated

   B. The best kind of leadership is: Authoritative, Socialist, Democratic

   C. The best way to get something done is: Form a committee, Do it yourself, Have others do it

4. Put your age in the upper right and corner.

5. Raise your left hand until recognized by the instructor.

6. **True** or **False:** (circle correct answer)

   A. A good leader always has an answer. It is a sign of weakness not to have an answer. T F

   B. A good leader should know how to follow directions. T F

   C. A good leader gets things done fast. T F

   D. It is better to do a job right rather than to do it quickly. T F

7. In question 6-B, underline the words "follow directions."

8. Stand up until recognized.

9. Define a leader (approximately 50 words) on the back of this page.

10. If you have read through this entire test as you were instructed to do, you don't have to take it. Just sign your name in the upper right hand corner and wait until the time is up. Do not answer questions 1 through 9.

LEG LIFT

Three guys are sent out of the room and brought back in one at a time. The object is to see which guy can lift his leg the highest while his other leg and shoulder are pressed firmly against the wall. It is impossible to do. You cannot lift your leg at all (Try it!). When the second guy comes in, tell him that the first guy got his leg up 32 inches high or something like that. He's got to top that to win. The result will be a very frustrated boy.

LEMON EATING RACE

Give three kids a raw lemon. On a signal, they must peel the lemon and eat all of it, not including the seeds and peel. First to finish wins.

LEMONADE EATING CONTEST

Get three guys to participate in a lemonade eating contest. The idea is that instead of mixing the lemonade first, the contestants will eat the ingredients, and it will mix on its own. They must first drink a large glass of water, eat a raw lemon, followed by a tablespoon of sugar. First guy to finish wins.

LETTER FROM CAMP

This is good for camps (naturally). Announce that you intercepted this letter at the post office and letters such as this are not allowed. The letter is below. Include some names of kids in the group to make it more fun.

Dear _____,

My week at camp is just about over. _____ is a nice place to camp—30,000,000 mosquitos can't be wrong. They told us that every room overlooked a beautiful canyon. They also overlooked inside toilets, mattresses and running water. My room is so small, the mice are hunchbacked. It does have a nice bath . . . I'd rather have a bed.

The cabin is modern—it has chrome doornobs, chrome bannisters, chrome windowsills—as a matter of fact, its the chromiest room I've ever been in. They have an Indian Village here. An old chief lives there and his name is Chief Running Water. He has three sons, Hot, Cold and Luke. When I visited there, Luke wasn't feeling so hot.

Really, this is the place for mosquitos. It's getting so you don't want to swat any of them because you don't want to kill your own flesh and blood. We got up early and went water skiing on the lake this morning. First time I ever went. I got behind the boat, on the skis, line in my hand—Then one ski went one way, the other went the other way and laugh . . . I thought I'd split! While I was recuperating the camp nurse, Heather, told me to drink a glass of warm milk after a hot bath. Dumb nurse, I couldn't ever finish drinking the hot bath.

Love, _____

LET'S GET ACQUAINTED

The following list should be printed up and given to each person in the group. The idea is to fill in each blank on your sheet with someone who fits the description. The first person to get all their blanks filled, or the one who has the most at the end of the time limit is the winner. The sample list below is only a suggested list. Be creative and come up with some of your own. This is a good way for kids to get to know each other a little better.

LET'S GET ACQUAINTED

1. Find someone who uses Listerine _____
2. Find someone who has three bathrooms in his house _____
3. Find someone who has gotten more than two traffic tickets _____
4. Find someone who has red hair _____
5. Find someone who gets hollered at for spending too much time in the bathroom _____
6. Find someone who has been inside the cockpit of an airplane _____
7. Find someone who plays a guitar _____
8. Find someone who likes "frog-legs" _____
9. Find someone who has been to Hawaii _____
10. Find someone who uses your brand of toothpaste _____
11. Find someone who has used an "outhouse" _____
12. Find a girl with false eyelashes on _____
13. Find a guy who has gone water skiing and got up the first time _____
14. Find someone who knows what "charisma" means _____
15. Find someone who is on a diet _____
16. Find a girl who uses a Lady Remington Shaver _____
17. Find a guy who has a match with him _____
18. Find someone who has his own private bath at home _____
19. Find someone who didn't know your last name _____
20. Find someone who has a funny sounding last name _____

LIPSTICK MASH

Using as many couples as you want, have the boys hold a tube of bright red lipstick in their mouths and attempt to apply it to the lips of their girl partners. The time limit is thirty seconds. When finished, the audience judges to determine the best job.

LONGJOHN STUFF

Select two girls and have them put on a pair of long underwear (preferably the kind that have the "trapdoor" in back). The girls should be wearing pants under them. Throw some balloons out into the audience and have the group blow up the balloons and tie them, then bat them up to the front. You will probably need a hundred or so balloons, depending on the size of the balloons. On a signal, two girl assistants begin stuffing the balloons into each of the other girls' longjohns. The balloons should be stuffed in the legs, the arms, and all over. The idea is to see which girl can get the most balloons in the longjohns in two minutes, so they have to work fast. At the end of the time period, have the girls count the balloons by popping them (while they are still in the longjohns) with a pin.

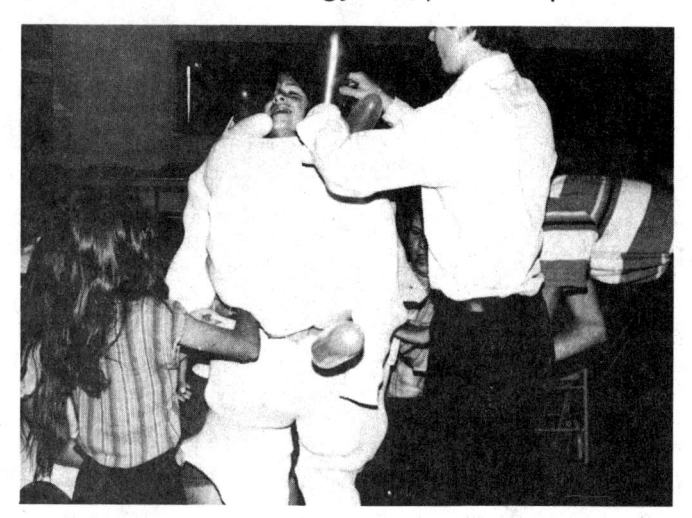

MAD LIBS

This game is a great crowd breaker for any age group, and is available in book form from most book stores (not Christian) and stationery stores. They are stories, with certain key words left out, such as nouns, adjectives, and persons, and the audience supplies the words as they are asked for by the leader, without knowing anything about the story. The words the audience supplies should be as ridiculous as possible, and the leader writes them into the story as provided in the "Mad Libs" book. The results are always entertaining.

MARSHMALLOW DROP

Select two or three couples for this event. Have the boys lie down on the floor and their girl partners are given marshmallows and a bowl of chocolate syrup. The girls must drop the marshmallows, dipped in the syrup, into the boys' open mouths, from at least waist high. The boys must catch the marshmallows in their mouths and eat them. The boy that eats the most is the winner. Deduct points for marshmallows that fall on the floor.

MONSTER MAKE-UP

Select three couples for this event. The boys sit in chairs facing the audience and the girls "make-up" the guys with "cosmetics" such as peanut butter, mud, toothpaste, and other messy items. The audience judges to determine the ugliest.

MOUTHWASH MYSTERY

Select three couples for this event. Tell the guys that each of their girlfriends will wash their mouths out with one of three different mouthwashes. They will then be blindfolded and by smelling the breath of each of the three girls, they must guess which is their girlfriend. Allow the guys to see which mouthwash their girlfriend will be using, and let them smell each to catch the scent of the mouthwash. Then blindfold the guys and send them out of the room. Substitute their girlfriends with three big guys and have each of these guys use the various mouthwashes. Bring the blindfolded boys in one at a time and have them smell the breath of each of the three other guys. Then ask them to identify their girlfriend. Ask them if they are absolutely sure that this is their girlfriend. After they have answered, let them remove the blindfold.

MUSICAL HATS

Pick six guys to stand in a circle, each facing the back of the guy in front. In other words, they would all be looking clockwise, or all counter-clockwise. Five of the guys put on hats (or you can use paper paint buckets) and on a signal (or when the music starts) each guy grabs the hat on the person's head in front of him and puts it on his own head. That way, the hats are moving around the circle from head to head until the next signal (or when the music stops). At that point, whoever is left without a hat is out of the game. Remove one hat and do it again until there are only two guys left. They stand back to back, grabbing the hat off of each others' head, and when the final signal is given, the one with the hat on is the winner.

MUSICAL MOTHER GOOSE

This is a good fun song that can be used with almost any age group. Teach it to the entire group (see music below) until everyone is familiar with the tune and the idea of the song. Then divide the group in half. Each side should have a leader who leads the group in the singing.

The song can be sung using the words to practically every "Mother Goose" rhyme there is. The ending is always the same, however, with the "they threw her (or him, etc.) out the window . . ." part. The first group begins with "Mary had a little lamb . . .," and when that group is finished, the other group starts singing the song only using a different nursery rhyme. The song goes back and forth until one of the groups cannot think of a new nursery rhyme. Whichever group gets stuck is the loser. There can be no pause between verses. Each verse must come in on time.

Some suggested rhymes: (There are a lot more)
    Mary Had a Little Lamb
    Old Mother Hubbard
    Humpty Dumpty
    Jack and Jill
    Little Jack Horner
    Hey Diddle Diddle

MUMMY

Select two or three guys to be "mummified." Each guy has two girls who wrap him up in toilet paper or paper towels from head to toe within a given time limit. The audience then judges to determine the best job.

NOBODY NOSE

Select four couples from the audience. The girls are sent out of the room and the guys stand behind a sheet which is hanging vertically and which has small holes in it. The boys are instructed to poke their noses through the holes in the sheet so that only their noses show on the front side of the sheet. The girls are then brought back into the room. They are not allowed to see behind the sheet, but they are shown the front of the sheet, with the noses exposed, only. The girls then must identify their boyfriends' noses by going up to the proper nose and kissing it. After all have done so, the sheet is lifted, and the girls can see if they have guessed properly.

Then, the game is reversed. The boys go out, and the girls stand behind the sheet. However, one of the girls is substituted with a boy from the audience. The guys come in and go through the same routine as the girls did, kissing the noses of their girlfriends. Due to the process of elimination, one of them will get a real surprise.

NOODLE WHOMP

First have two girls get down on all fours, facing each other, with blindfolds on. They should join left hands. Each girl has a rolled up newspaper, and gets three tries to hit the other girl with it. The girl being swung at may move anywhere to try and get out of the way, but cannot move her left hand. Whichever girl gets hit the most times is the loser. Try it next with a pair of boys. Lastly, have a championship with the boy winner playing the girl winner. After the blindfolds are on, take the blindfold off of the girl. The boy will get clobbered.

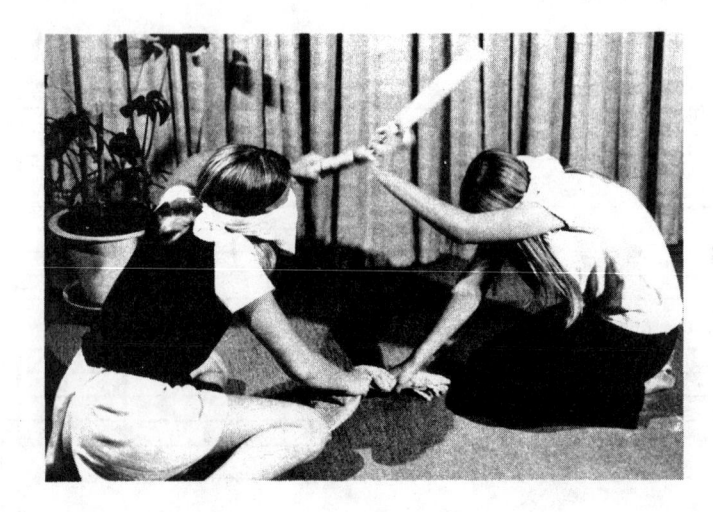

NOSE ART

Have easels at the front of the room with drawing paper attached. Select three volunteers who must "paint" on the drawing paper with poster paint applied with their noses. Have the audience judge to determine the winner.

NOSE BALANCE

The participants sit on chairs facing the audience. They are to lean their heads back. A penny is placed on their nose. The object is to wiggle the penny off their noses **without moving their heads.** First to knock the penny off wins.

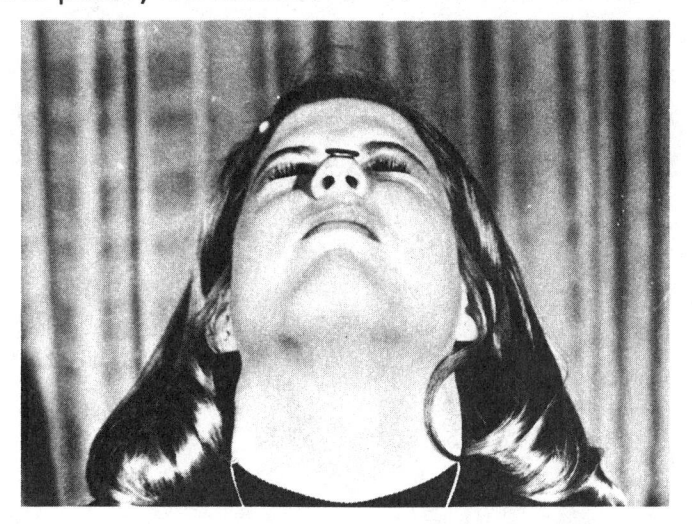

NYLON RACE

Select two guys and and have them come to the front and be seated in chairs, facing the audience. Each are given a pair of nylon stockings and a pair of garden gloves. With the gloves on, they race to see who can put the nylons on in the fastest time. Shoes must be taken off.

OBSTACLE COURSE

Challenge several guys to walk blindfolded through an obstacle course of some kind. Offer a good prize if they can do it. Send the participants out of the room and bring them in one at a time to try it. Blindfold him after he has had a chance to see the obstacles. Then remove all the obstacles. It is really funny to watch.

ONION ON A STICK

Choose three volunteers to play this little game. They line up about 20 feet away from a table which has three carameled apples on it. On a signal, the guys are to run to the table and eat a carameled apple. The first person to completely eat the apple they pick up is the winner. What they are not aware of, however, is that one of the apples if really a carameled *onion*.

PATCH SEW

Choose three couples who come to the front of the room. The girls are seated and the guys lay across the lap of their girl partner, face to the floor. The girls are given napkins and a needle and thread. The object is to see which girl can sew all four corners of the napkins on their boy partner's seat in the fastest time (and without sticking their partner with the needle).

PEOPLE BINGO

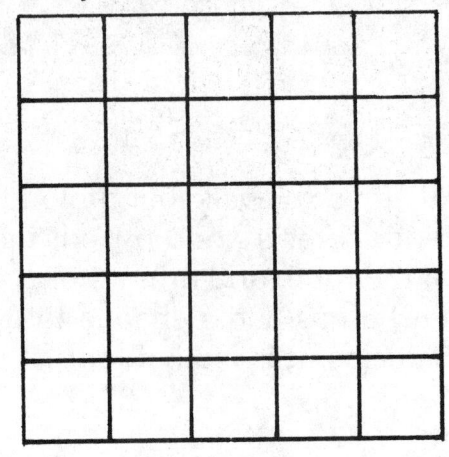

Randomly select people's names to fill in each square on playing boxes below (one name to a square). The best way to do this is to give every kid a playing card like the one illustrated below that is blank, then each kid just looks around the room and puts somebody's name in every square. Then, from a hat, randomly pull kid's names and if a player has that kids name on his card, he marks an "X" through that name. The first person who has a row of "X's" either horizontally, vertically, or diagonally, wins.

PING PONG FLOUR BLOW

Have two boys compete to see who can blow a ping pong ball out of a round bowl in the fastest time. Each try and are timed. Then, to make it even harder, they are to try it blindfolded. The first boy does and is timed. Then the second boy tries. But just before he blows, dump a cup of flour in the bowl.

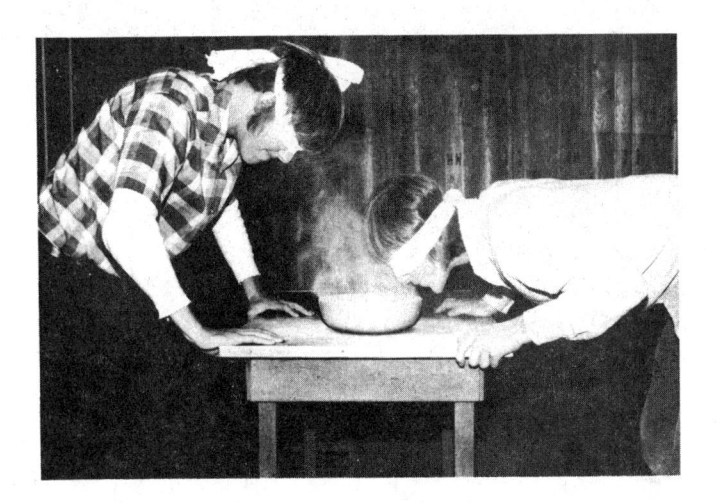

PING-PONG BALL RACE

Select several kids to race ping-pong balls. Each player gets a party blower (the type that uncoils when you blow it) and they push the balls across the floor using those blowers only. They cannot blow directly on the ball or touch it in any way. First across the finish line wins.

PLATE HYPNOTISM

Explain to the audience that you have had some experience in college with hypnotism. You learned a relatively obscure method of hypnotism called "Plate Hypnotism." Ask if there is anyone in the group who would like to be hypnotised. Usually you will get someone to volunteer, as most of the kids don't really believe you can do it anyway. Ask your volunteer to sit down. Give him (or her) a plate to hold in his hand. (It must be a ceramic or china plate). He must hold it by the edge, perfectly level so that the "magic power" won't spill out of the plate, and with his left hand. Then you sit across from him, facing him, about 10 feet away. You also have a plate and your volunteer is instructed to stare directly into your eyes, and do everything that you do, except talking. You also ask the audience to be as quiet as possible. You then begin by taking your finger (right hand) and rubbing the top of the plate, then rubbing it between your eyes. Do this over and over while saying something like, "We're getting the hypnotic power from the top of the plate and rubbing it into the eyes . . . You are getting sleepier and sleepier . . ." After a few moments of this, you move to the edges of the plate with your finger, then finally you rub the bottom of the plate. The volunteer should be doing the same. You continue the chatter: "Now we are getting hypnotic power from the bottom of the plate and rubbing it around our eyes . . . Your eyes are getting heavier and sleepier . . ." This is where the fun begins. Beforehand, you have charred the bottom of the volunteer's plate with a match, so that as he rubs the bottom of the plate, then his eyes, he is smearing black soot all over his face. He is not aware of this, because he is staring you straight in the eyes and cannot see his finger. Continue until he catches on, then show him a mirror.

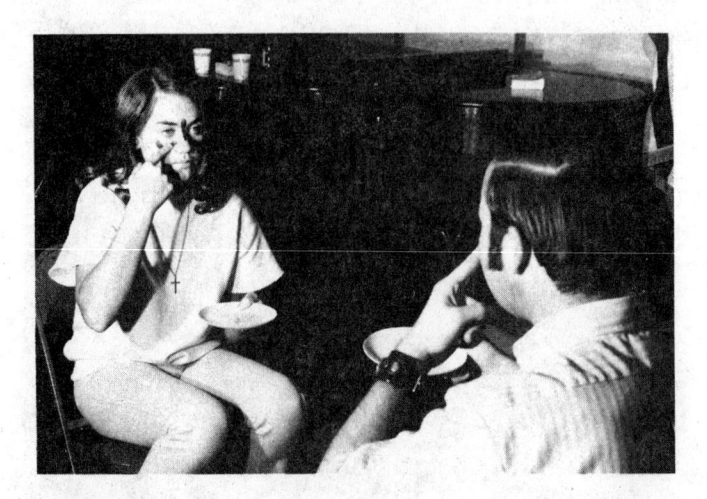

POKER CHIP PUSHUPS

Choose two guys from the audience who think that they are the athletic type. Explain to them that they are going to compete to see who can do a **pushup** in the fastest time. The only thing is, that while they are in the "down" position of the pushup, they must, with their mouths, stack three poker chips (or checkers, etc.) that have been placed on the floor under their faces, one on top of the other, and then rise to a full "up" position. They must not touch their bodies to the floor in any way.

Have each guy try it once for practice and then have them do it again for time. Decide who the winner is, and then tell them, ". . . we'll give the loser another chance to win. This time we'll do exactly the same thing, only we'll blindfold each of you so that you won't be able to see the poker chips." Assure them that you won't steal the chips out from under them, but that they will remain in the same position. (Let them feel the poker chips before they try it.) Have the loser of the first try go first. Time him and then let the second guy try. Get him all set, and give him the count-down (as you did for the first guy), and just before you say "go," place a whipped cream pie on top of the poker chips. He will be in such a hurry to get to the chips, this his face will land right in the pie.

Caution:
(1) Do not use shaving cream. Contestant will smell it.
(2) Use a different set of poker chips for each guy.
(3) Build this up as an athletic contest, and don't let it appear to be a "gag" or "stunt," or it may bomb.

POP BOTTLE PICKUP

Select several boys to see who can stand on one foot, with the other foot held up with his hand, and try to pick up a standing pop bottle with his teeth. Whoever can do it in the shortest time wins. If you fall over, you're out.

POPCORN STUFF

Select three couples for this event. Ask for the girls with the biggest mouths. Each guy gets a bag of popcorn, and one at a time, they try to see how many popped kernels of popcorn they can stuff in their girl partner's mouth. Count them one at a time as they go in. No swallowing is allowed. Give an appropriate prize to the winning couple. You may also do this event with grapes instead of popcorn.

PSYCHOLOGICAL SIT-UPS

Explain to the group that while you were in college you studied "Psycho-cybernetics," and learned how to create mental blocks that could prevent even the strongest men from doing something as simple as a "sit-up." Just to prove your point, you choose a "volunteer" from the audience. You ask him to lie down (on a table top so that the audience can see) and just for practice, do a simple sit-up. When he does, have the audience give him a hand. Then you explain how you are going to create the "mental block." He must lie flat on his back, hands at his side, and his eyes must be closed. He is to concentrate on doing a sit-up. ON A SIGNAL, THE AUDIENCE WILL BEGIN YELLING, CLAPPING, STOMPING THEIR FEET and making as much noise as possible. While this is going on, you will be yelling "You can't sit up! You can't sit up!" at the volunteer. After about 15 seconds of this, you cut off the audience noise (with a wave of your hand) and the volunteer is to immediately try to sit up. He won't be able to.

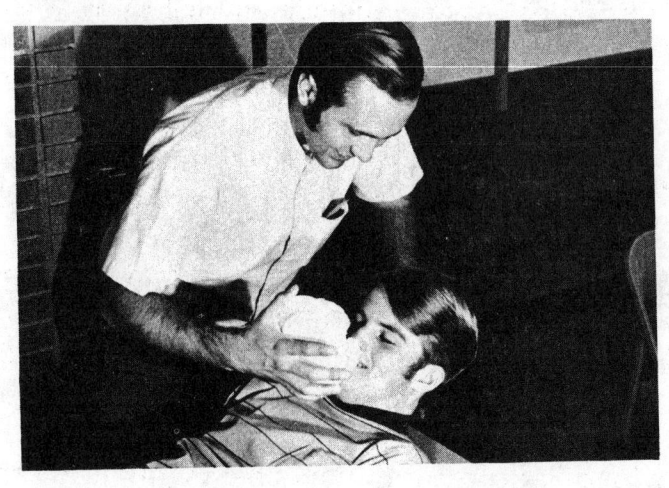

So you try this, going through all the steps above, and sure enough, your volunteer just lies there, grunts and groans, but can't sit up. The reason, of course, is that he is clued in ahead of time, and he is merely acting. But what that does is make all the guys in the audience want to try it, because they don't believe it is possible, and they want to prove that you are a phony. So, choose another volunteer who is sure that he can sit up and prove you wrong, and invite him to come forward and lie down like the first volunteer. Make sure he understands the rules (hands at side, eyes closed), otherwise the experiment won't work. Have him do a practice sit-up, like before, and go through the whole routine. This time, while the audience is yelling and you are shouting "You can't sit-up!, etc.," an assistant hands you a cream pie (made with "Crazy Foam" or shaving soap, etc.). When you cut off the audience noise, your volunteer quickly will sit up with no problem at all. You just hold the pie in front of his face, and when he sits up, SPLAT! The results are always funny, and your volunteer usually feels a little embarrassed at being such a sucker. Be sure and provide a towel for him to wipe his face off with.

PSYCHOLOGICAL STORY

Three people are sent out of the room, and you explain that you are going to tell each volunteer a story, one at a time. The story is a symbolic one, and only the audience is clued in as to what the symbols in the story mean. The symbols are:

1. The Forest. It represents life. In other words, if a person sees his forest as dark and gloomy, then that would be his outlook on life.
2. The Cup. It represents religion.
3. The Key. It represents education.
4. The Bear. It represents life's problems.
5. The Water. It represents sex.
6. The Wall. It represents death.

The story is then told to the volunteers as you bring them back into the room one at a time. Explain to each that they are to use their imagination and be as creative and as descriptive as possible as they follow your instructions. The story should go something like this:

> "Imagine that you are in a forest. What does your imaginary forest look like? (Wait for their response.) You begin walking down a trail in the forest and you find a key lying in the trail. Describe the key and tell us what you decide to do with it. (Response.) You go a little farther down the trail and you find a cup. Describe the cup and tell us what you do with it. (Response.) You continue down the trail and suddenly you reach some water. What does the water look like, and what is your response to it? (Response.) A short while later you find a bear. Describe the bear, what it does, and what you do. (Response) Last of all you encounter a wall. Describe the wall and what you do on finding the wall. What is on the other side of the wall? (Response.)"

After each person has been told the story and they have responded, then you can let them in on the meaning of the symbols. It is also wise to explain that this was done only for fun, and there is really no significance to the symbolism and the various responses. All it means is you have a very active imagination. This crowd-breaker is good for a lot of laughs, and works best with high school students or older.

QUESTION AND ANSWER GAME

Hand out plain cards and pencils to everyone in group. Divide into two teams. Everyone on team 1 will write a question beginning with "how" such as "how do you peel a prune?" Everyone on the other team will write an answer beginning with "by" such as "by using pinking shears." Collect the cards, keeping them in two groups, and then read first a question and then an answer. Random reading will produce hilarious results.

QUICK-DRAW CONTEST

Place an easel with a drawing pad on it at the front of the room. Choose two couples, and send them out of the room. The guy stands at the easel with a felt tip pen and the girl faces the audience and is given an object, such as a can opener, a light bulb, a screwdriver, etc. (The guy should not see what the object is.) The girl then tries to describe the object to the boy and the boy tries to draw it from her description, and guess what the object is. The girl cannot use words that would give away what the object is, but must merely describe the shape of it, such as "Draw a straight line about three inches long, and then curve it slightly to the right . . ." With younger kids, allow the girl to watch the boy as he draws, and give him instructions, correcting, etc. Time the first couple and then bring the second couple in and they do the same thing with the same object. Don't make the object **too** hard.

REVOLVING STORY

Begin at one side of the room or circle. The first person begins to make up a fairy tale of some kind. He continues for 10 seconds and at a signal the next person in line adds to the story for 10 seconds and so on down the line. The results are usually quite funny.

RIDE THE TUB

For this game, you will need to get an old washtub big enough to stand in. Through the two handles of the tub (over the top of the tub) a six foot long pole or pipe is placed. The two ends of the pole are then placed on the seats of two chairs so that the tub hangs suspended between the two chairs. Next, hang four hats on the backs of the chairs, two on each chair. Select three boys to, one at a time, stand in the tub with one leg on each side of the pole, and with a broom, knock the hats off of the chair. They must balance themselves in the tub without holding on to anything and knock the hats down before they fall out of the tub, which inevitably happens. The guy that gets the most hats off is the winner.

ROMEO

For this crowd-breaker, you will need a telephone in your meeting room. Have a guy, who considers himself to be a real "ladies man," call a girl at random and try to get a date with her. He has three minutes to do so. If he is successful, the date will be paid for by you. You make the phone call (supposedly to avoid "cheating" by the guy) and you call a girl who has been clued-in and is ready to make up all kinds of excuses why she can't go on the date. The result will be a very frustrated boy.

Another twist to this would be to go ahead and let the guy call any girl he wants (other than his steady girlfriend) and ask her to go with him on some terrible date, such as helping him write a term paper on "The economic development of East Pakistan," or to help clean out his basement, etc. If the girl accepts, they get dinner for two as a prize.

RUBBER BAND RELAY

Use three guys in this "face co-ordination" test. Place a rubber band around each guy's head with it crossing over the tip of his nose. The idea then, is to maneuver the rubber band from the nose down to the neck without using hands. Any facial contortion he can think of is legal.

RUSSIAN ROULETTE FOR CHICKEN-HEARTS

Hard boil four eggs and leave one raw (total of 5 eggs). Then color them with food coloring. Call up five boys, each getting to choose the egg that they want broken on top of their heads. One guy picks the raw egg and things get a little messy. For best results, have 5 girls stand behind the guys and at a signal, all 5 girls break the eggs simultaneously on each boys' head.

SHOE STRETCH

Get two old pair of men's shoes. Take out the shoestrings, punch a hole in the back of the shoes, and tie a four foot piece of elastic to each shoe. Place two chairs about twenty feet apart or so and tie the other ends of the elastic to the legs of the chairs. (One pair of shoes on each chair.) Now get two boy volunteers to play the game. The boys each put on a pair of the shoes (they are not tied, but loose on their feet) and the boys are to walk to each other, stretching the elastic, and exchange shoes without using their hands. Have people sitting in the two chairs to weight them. If the shoes snap back to the chair, the player must start over from there. Have several two-man teams compete to see which can do it in the fastest time.

SHOE TIE

Select three couples to play this game. The boys should be wearing shoes that have shoestrings (not boots, etc.). The boys are seated and one of their shoes is untied. The girls must re-tie the shoe using one hand and anything else (except the other hand). The girl to finish first wins.

SHOULDER PIN

Have two kids come to the front, sit on the floor back to back and lock arms. On a signal, they each try to pin the other's right shoulder to the floor. It's sort of like Indian arm wrestling, only using your whole body.

THE SIT DOWN GAME

This is a good crowd breaker that is always fun and requires very little preparation and no props. It involves everyone. Simply have everyone stand up. Announce that you will be reading of a list of "if" characteristics and if the "if" characteristic applies to them, they must sit down. For example, you might say, "Sit down if you are ugly." Each person must decide if that description fits them, and if so, then they must sit down and remain seated. That's really all there is to it. What makes the game funny is how creative you are at coming up with the "if" characteristics. Here are a few examples of good ones that you might want to use, but you should try to throw in some original ones of your own.

> You didn't use a deodorant today.
> You have worn the same socks for two days.
> Your belly-button is an "outie."
> You went to the drive-in last weekend (but didn't see the movie).
> You dated a loser last week.
> You have a zit on your nose.
> You are a girl and have a run in your nylon.
> You are a boy and have a run in YOUR nylon.
> You read this month's issue of PLAYBOY.
> You WISH you could read this month's issue of PLAYBOY.
> You still suck your thumb.
> You have dandruff.
> You weigh over 200 pounds.
> Your nose is running.
> You are really good looking.
> STAND UP if the person next to you just sat down and was wrong.
> You have never eaten snail.
> Your mother dresses you.
> The person next to you smells bad.
> You have a hole in your sock.
> Your fly is open.
> You recently got a traffic ticket.
> You are on a diet.
> You're not a diet, but you should be.
> You have false teeth.
> You are mad at your boyfriend or girlfriend right now.

End with one like "Sit down if you are tired of standing," or something like that, and that will usually get everyone down.

THE SITUATION GAME

If you have your group sitting around in a circle, or in rows of chairs, this makes a fun game to liven things up. Have everybody whisper in the ear of the person to their right WHO THEY ARE. Have everybody be as creative as possible with this, and tell the person that they (the person getting told) are Batman, Brigitte Bardot, etc. Then have everybody tell the person to their left WHERE THEY ARE. These should also be funny, such as "in the bathtub," "on top of a flagpole," etc. Then have everybody mix up and find new seats, and tell the person to the right of them WHAT THEY ARE WEARING. Then have everybody tell the person to their left WHAT THEY ARE DOING. After all this is done, have each person tell who they are, where they are, what they are wearing, and what they are doing. (They tell the things that the other people told them.) Such as, "My name is Phyllis Diller, I'm wearing a purple bikini, and I'm in the bathroom, doing pushups." If you have a large crowd, appoint only a few to tell their story or ask for a few volunteers.

SKYDIVING LESSON

Three boys are chosen to learn how to skydive. One at a time, each boy is brought into the room and asked to stand on a sturdy 2 x 4 plank, which is lifted up by 2 strong boys. He uses the leaders' shoulders as a brace, so he won't fall. The board is lifted up about 3 feet, then the contestant is asked to jump into a small circle for five points. The board is lifted higher, and he jumps again for 10 points. The last times, for 20 points, he must jump blindfolded. The strong boys, however, only lift the board 2 or 3 inches, and the leader stoops down real low, giving the blindfolded contestant the feeling that he is high. He jumps, but usually falls flat on his face.

SOAP SCULPTURE

Give three couples (or three individuals) each a can of "Crazy Foam" (available in most toy stores) or shaving cream. They shoot a big glob of soap out onto the table, or onto a plate and get two minutes to "sculpture" it into anything they want. The audience judges the best job.

SPAGHETTI HAIRDOS

Have several couples come forward and give each a bowl of wet (cold) spaghetti. The boys sit in chairs facing the audience, and the girls stand behind the boys. The girls get one minute to dump the bowl of spaghetti on the boys' heads and arrange it into a "spaghetti hairdo." The girl that does the best job on her boy wins. The audience judges.

SPEECH SPASM

Have a volunteer come to the front and announce that he is going to be tested to see if he can earn a dollar bill. All he has to do is say two common, simple words: "Toy" and "Boat." He must say the two words ten times in five seconds *correctly* and he gets the dollar bill. Have him try the words separately to make sure he can pronounce them. (Have the audience applaud.) Then have him try it quickly as instructed. It is highly unlikely that he will be able to.

SQUIRT GUN DUEL

Blindfold two guys and have a squirt gun fight. Before you start it, however, remove one guy's blindfold.

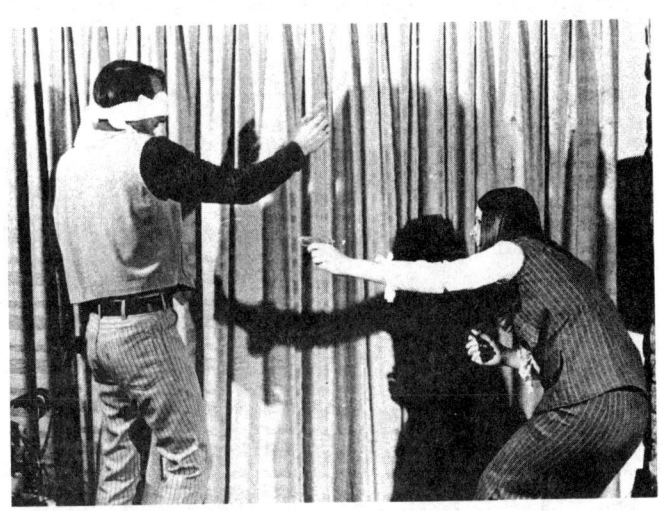

STANDING BROAD GRIN

Ask for all the "big mouths" in the group to come forward. Give a prize to whoever can "grin" the widest grin. Use a ruler to determine the winner, and give him a tube of toothpaste, or a bottle of mouthwash as a prize.

SUBMARINE RIDE

A volunteer lays flat on a table with a person at each arm and each leg. The legs are the left and right rudders. The arms are Torpedo One and Torpedo Two. A jacket is put over the volunteer's head with one sleeve directly on his nose. This is the periscope. The captain (you or the leader) yells "Left Rudder!" (Person on left leg raises leg) "Right Rudder!" (raise right leg) "Torpedo One!" "Torpedo Two!" (raise arms) "Up Periscope!" (Sleeve is lifted straight up.) "Dive! Dive!" (You pour water down sleeve and into the volunteer's face.)

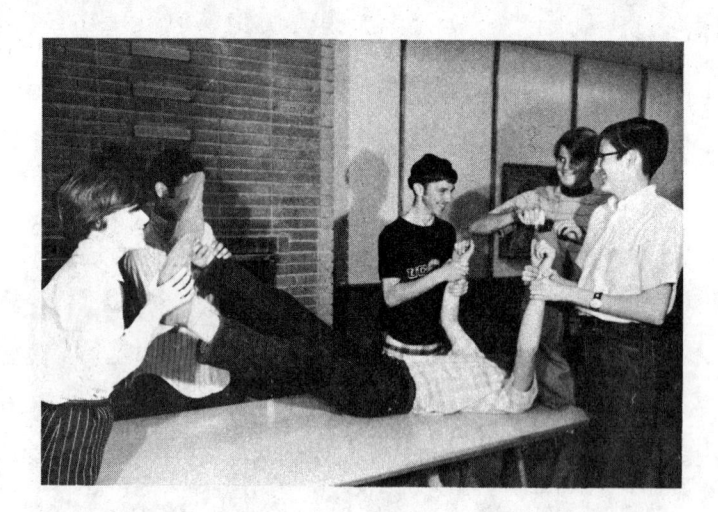

TAKE OFF WHAT YOU DON'T NEED

Have a guy come up, lie down on a table, and cover him with a blanket. Tell him to take off something that he doesn't need, and toss it off of the table. He will usually take off something like his shoes, or a wrist watch. You continue to ask him to take off something that he doesn't need, and he will continue to do so until he refuses to take off anything else. The idea is to get him to take off the **blanket,** since he doesn't really need it. He will make all kinds of excuses as to why he can't take anything else off, but you insist that he can. If he doesn't catch on, and has to be told, award a penalty of some kind . . .

A good variation of this old trick is to do it with three guys, bringing them into the room one at a time to go through the same gag. The last guy is clued in and has on a pair of swimming trunks under his pants. He will take off everything (except for the swimming trunks which the audience doesn't know about), which of course is a surprise to the audience. He then throws the blanket off, and that's when the girls all start screaming.

TAXATION WITHOUT REPRESENTATION

Tell a volunteer that you will give him a quarter if he can say "Taxation without Representation" ten times in ten seconds. He will try it, saying the phrase rapidly, but probably goofing it up. It is very difficult. However, the trick is to simply say "Taxation" ten times. That is, in reality, what you want him to do: to say "Taxation" without saying "Representation." Try it on several kids and see if any can get it.

TEN TOES ON THE ROCKS

Fill two pans with crushed ice and place ten marbles in the bottom of the pans, underneath the ice. Two boys must remove their shoes and socks and try to get the marbles out of the pan using their toes only. They cannot turn the pan over, or spill any ice. The first to get all the marbles out of the pan is the winner.

THREAD THE NEEDLE

Call three guys up to see who can thread the needle with one eye closed in the fastest time. Give the first guy the needle and thread, appoint a timekeeper, and to assure that he will only use one eye, you will put your hand over one of his eyes. Give each guy two tries, using one eye and then the other. On the last guy, smear some lipstick or soot on your hand, and smear it all over the last guy's eyes when you put your hand over his eyes. (Use a large needle or this will take too long.)

TOMATO TEST

Have three couples compete in this little game. Each couple places a tomato between their foreheads, and while holding it there with no hands, the girl tries to put a shoe on the boy's foot. It would not be wise to do this one on a carpeted floor.

TOOTHPASTE CATCH

Have three volunteers lay on the floor, face up, with a small paper cup in each of their mouths. Their partners stand and try to fill the cup with toothpaste by squeezing it out of the tube and letting it drop from at least three feet up. Give the winner a toothbrush.

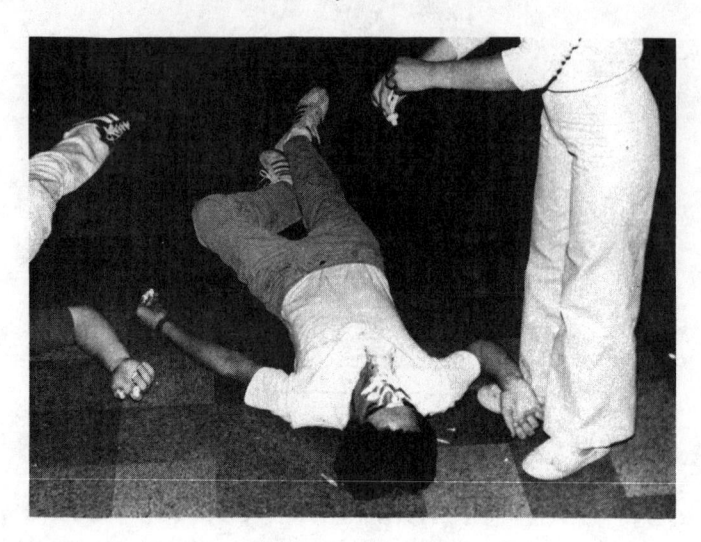

UN-BANANA

Select three guys who race to see who can peel a banana, eat it, then drink a bottle of Seven-Up the fastest. Watch their mouths foam up. Give the winner a bunch of bananas and a six-pack of Seven-Up.

THE W.C.

This is a crowd breaker which is simply read to the group. Give the following background information, then read the letter which follows:

An English lady while visiting in Switzerland was looking for a room and she asked the school-master if he could recommend one. He took her to see several rooms, and when everything was settled, the lady returned home to make final preparations to move. When she arrived home, the thought occurred to her that she had not seen a "W.C." in the place. (A W.C. is a "water closet" or a bathroom.)

So she immediately wrote a note to the school-master asking him if there was a W.C. in the place. The school-master was a very poor student in English, so he asked the Parish Priest if he could help in the matter. Together they tried to find the meaning of the letters, W.C. The only solution they could find for the letters was "Wayside Chapel." The school-master then wrote the following letter to the English lady:

> My Dear Madam:
>
> I take great pleasure in informing you that the W.C. is situated nine miles from the house in the center of a beautiful grove of pine trees surrounded by lovely grounds.
>
> It is capable of holding 229 people, and it is open on Sundays and Thursdays only. As there are a great number of people expected during the summer months, I suggest that you come early, although usually there is plenty of standing room. This is an unfortunte situation, especially if you are in the habit of going regularly. It may be of some interest to know that my daughter was married in the W.C. and it was there that she met her husband. I can remember the rush there was for seats. There were 10 people to every seat usually occupied by one. It was wonderful to see the expressions on their faces.
>
> You will be glad to hear that a good number of people bring their lunch and make a day of it, while those who can afford to go by car, arrive just on time. I would especially recommend your ladyship to go on Thursdays when there is an organ accompaniment. The acoustics are excellent, and even the most delicate sounds can be heard everywhere.
>
> The newest addition is a bell donated by a wealthy resident of the district. It rings everytime a person enters. A bazaar is to be held to provide for plush seats for all, since the people feel it is long needed. My wife is rather delicate so she cannot attend regularly. It is almost a year since she went last, and naturally it pains her very much not to be able to go more often.
>
> I shall be delighted to reserve the best seat for you, where you shall be seen by all. For the children, there is a special day and time so that they do not disturb the elders. Hoping to be of some service to you,
>
> The School Master

WALK THE PLANK

A board is placed on the floor, and an obstacle of some sort is placed at the end of the plank. You blindfold a victim, and have him "walk the plank," and jump over the obstacle at the end of it. Only you remove the obstacle before he gets to it. So he jumps over a non-existent object.

WATER BALLOON SHAVE

Three couples come to the front of the room. The boys sit in chairs facing the audience and hold a large water balloon on their heads. Their girl partners cover the balloons with shaving cream, and with a single edged razor blade (no razor, just the blade) try to "shave" all the soap off of the balloon without breaking it. Whoever is the first to succeed is the winner.

WATER EGGS

A "Water Egg" is just like a water balloon, except that you fill an egg with water instead of a balloon. This is done by poking a small hole in each of the two ends of the egg, then emptying its contents by either blowing or sucking on one end. Plug one end with wax (paraffin) and fill the egg with water through the other end. Then plug that hole with wax. The result is a "Water Egg." Use your imagination on how to use them.

WEIGHT GUESSING CONTEST

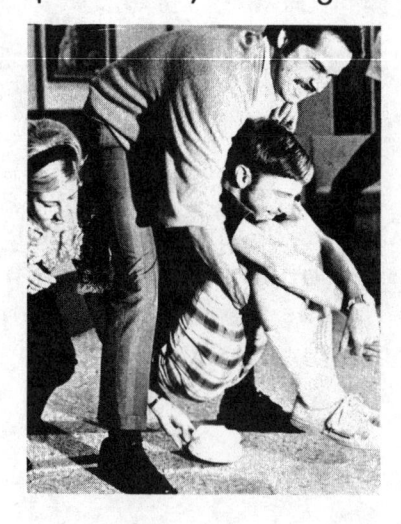

Make a big speech to the group about how great you are at guessing people's weight. Explain that you can guess anyone's weight within two pounds just by picking them up off the ground. Ask for volunteers. Three people volunteer, but two of them you have secretly talked to beforehand, so you know what their weight is. Those two go first. They sit down on the floor, and you pick them straight up (your hands under their knees), and to the amazement of all, you guess their weights perfectly. Now it's the "sucker's" turn. He sits down on the floor, you pick him up, and while you are holding him up in the air, an assistant slips a cream pie underneath the guy's seat. You then just drop him into the pie.

WHISTLE AND BURP

Select two couples to participate in this one. The boys get five saltine crackers and the girls get a small bottle of Coke. On a signal, the boys must eat the crackers and whistle, and the girls must drink the Coke and burp. The first to do it wins.

WHO HIT ME?

Have two guys lie down on the floor (face up, side by side) and put a blanket over them so that they cannot see. All the crowd forms a circle around them, and one person in the crowd has a rolled up newspaper. The newspaper is passed around to someone who takes it and hits one of the guys under the blanket on the head with it, then gets back into the circle, leaving the newspaper on the blanket. The guy who has been hit counts to 10 and comes out from the blanket and tries to guess who hit him. If he guesses correctly, the person who is guessed goes under the blanket in his place.

These are the instructions given to the crowd and to the players. However, one of the guys under the blanket has been "clued in" ahead of time that **he** will be given the newspaper and he will reach over and smack the guy laying next to him with it, then pull his arm in under the blanket real fast and play dumb. The guy who is hit will jump up, and his guesses will always be wrong. (Hit the clued-in guy once in a while so that it won't look quite so rigged.)

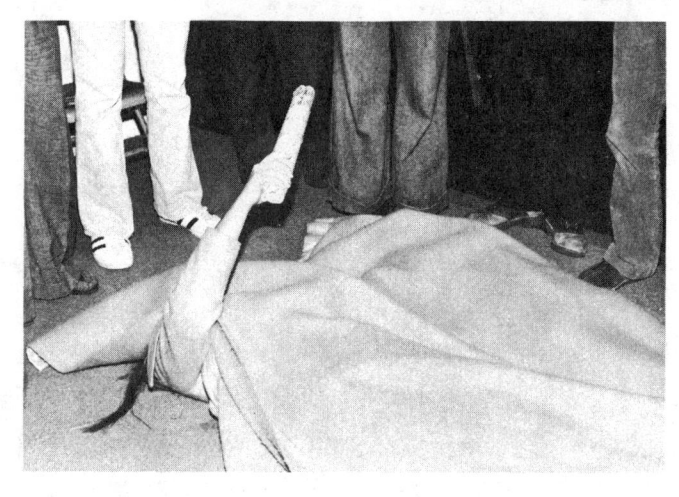

WILLIAM TELL

Make "Candle Hats" by either putting candles on top of real hats, or by putting candles on the bottom of saucers, then tying the saucers on a person's head with ribbon. Use your own creativity here. The important thing is to get candles on top of a person's head.

Next, give the players squirt guns, and with the candles lit on their heads, they try to put out the other's candle by squirting it out. They cannot move their feet. The idea is simply to keep your candle lit and put out your opponent's.

A variation of this would be to use couples. The guys wear the candles on their heads and the girls get the squirt guns. Each couple stands about ten feet apart. On a signal, the girls try to put out the candle on their boyfriend's head with the squirt gun. The first to do so wins.

WRAP THE DUCK

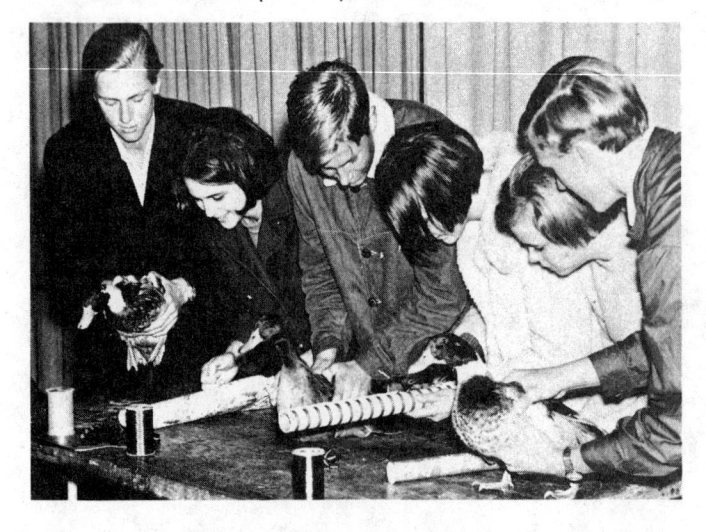

This is a great Christmas party idea, if you have access to some live ducks. Have couples compete to see which can "gift wrap" a duck the best in a two minute (or so) time limit. Provide wrapping paper, ribbon, tape, etc., but no boxes. Make sure that the kids do not hurt the ducks (squashing them or whatever) and this can be really fun to watch. Other animals work just as well, such as chickens or rabbits. Have the rest of the group decide who is the winning couple.

Chapter Two

Games

AMERICAN EAGLE

This is not a co-ed game. Guys and gals should play separately. All guys line up on a line. They choose one who stands 30 feet or so away (in the middle of a field). When the whistle is blown, players start running toward the guy in the middle of the field. That guy tackles one (or more if he can), and has to hold him down and say "American Eagle" three times. The rest of the players now are on the other side of the field, and now must run through 2 guys to get back to the original side again. This keeps up until everybody has been tackled and are in the middle of the field, and there are no more guys to run across. Give a prize to whoever lasts the longest.

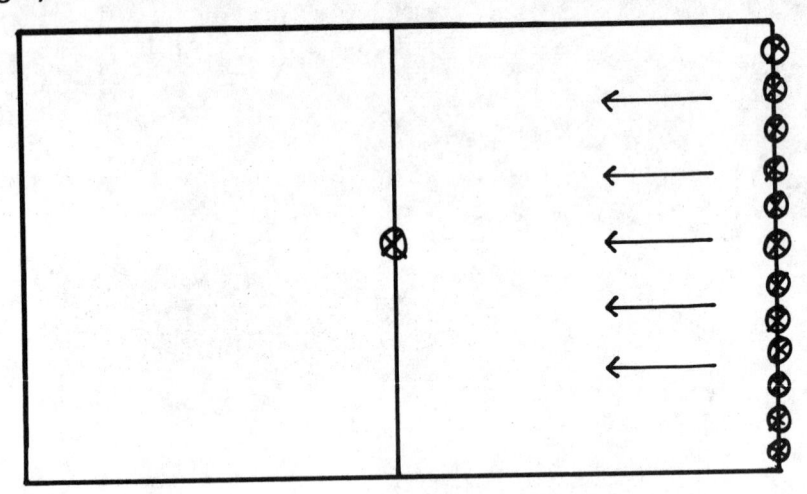

AMOEBA

Divide into teams and simply tie a rope around the team at their waists. To do this, have the team bunch up as close together as they can, and hold their hands up in the air while you tie the rope around them. After they are tied, they can race to a goal and back. Unless they work together and cooperate as a team, they will go nowhere. This is a good fun game for camps and outdoor activities.

ANATOMY SHUFFLE

This game is similar to "Birdie on the Perch." The group pairs off, and forms two circles, one inside the other. One member of each couple is on the inside circle, the other is in the outside circle.

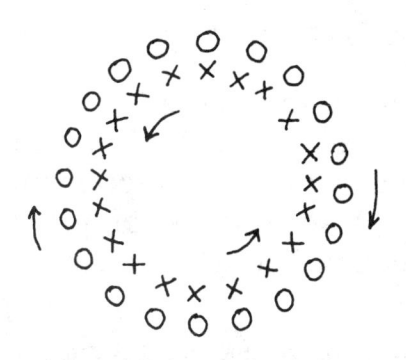

The outer circle begins travelling in one direction (clockwise), and the inner circle goes in the opposite direction (counter-clockwise). The leader blows a whistle and yells out something like "Hand, Ear!" On this signal, the inner circle group must find their partners and place their hand on their partner's ear. Last couple to do so is out of the game. The leader calls out all sorts of combinations as the game progresses, such as:

"Finger, Foot"   "Nose, shoulder"
"Thigh, Thigh"   "Head, stomach"
"Elbow, nose"   "Nose, Armpit"

The first thing called is always the inner group's part of the body, and they must find their partners, who stand in one position (they cannot move after the whistle blows) and touch their part of the body to the second item called on the partner. The last couple to remain in the game wins.

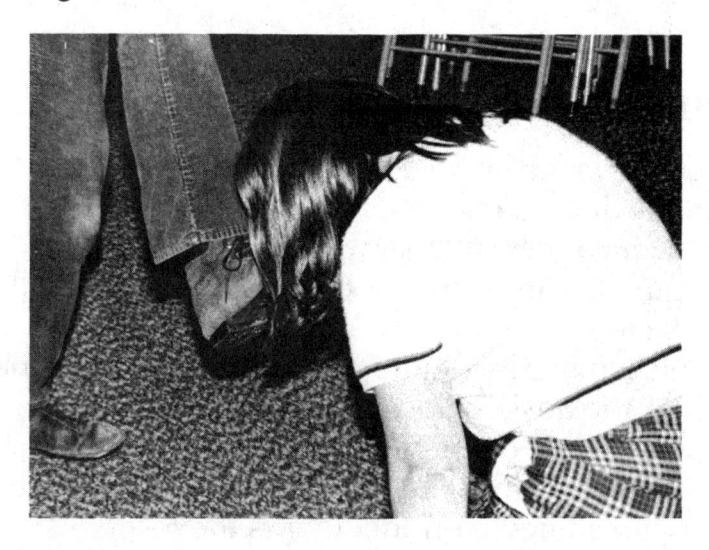

ART CHARADES

Teams play "charades" using the titles of pop songs (current hits) as titles to be guessed. Instead of "acting out" or using hand signals and pantomime, each player uses a piece of poster board and felt tip pins to describe the song title. No words can be used. Have each team select its "artist" and complete for fastest time.

BALLOON BASKETBALL

Arrange your chairs in the following manner. There should be the same number of people on each of the two teams that are playing. One team faces in one direction, the second team faces the other direction. There can be any number of players on a team, just so long as the teams are equal. The two rows of chairs on each end should face inward.

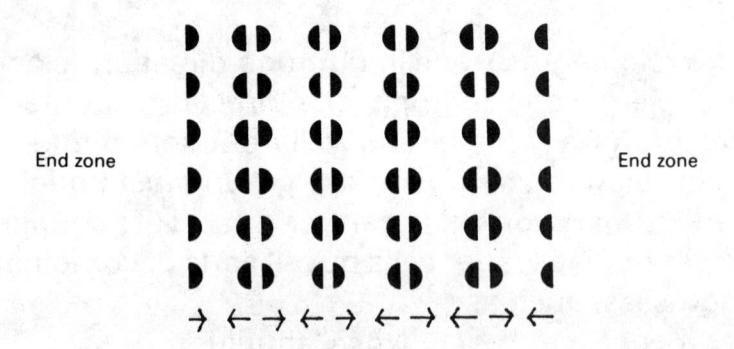

End zone   End zone

After all the players are seated in their team's chairs, toss a balloon into the center of the players. The players cannot stand, but they must try to "bat" the balloon to the end zone that they are facing with their hands. As soon as the balloon drops into the end zone over the heads of the last row of people, the team going that direction wins 2 points. If the balloon goes out of bounds, just throw it back into the center. Play can be to 20 points, or may end after 15 minutes of play.

BALLOON BUST

This is a good way to choose couples for a game like "Birdie on the Perch" or any other game that requires couples. All the girls, or half the group (which is best) each get a piece of paper and a balloon. They write their names on the pieces of paper and then put them inside the balloons, blow up the balloons, and tie them. All the balloons are placed in the middle of the room. On a signal, the half of the group (or the boys) whose names are not in the balloons, grab a balloon, pop it, read the name on the piece of paper inside, and try to locate the person whose name they have. The last couple to locate each other and sit down on the floor is the loser.

BUMPER BOX RELAY

For this relay, you need to obtain a large refrigerator box for each team. Each player then gets inside the box, standing up, with the box over his head and the open end of the box down to the floor. On a signal, the players then race to the opposite wall or goal and back while receiving directions from their teammates who must yell them out from behind the starting line. Since the players cannot see, they run into each other, go the wrong way, and the results are really funny. For an added dimension to this game, decorate the boxes with wild colors, team names, or whatever.

BALLOON POP RELAY

Divide the group into teams. The teams line up single file at a starting line. A chair is placed about 30 feet away. Each team member has a deflated balloon. One at a time, kids run to the chair, blow up balloon, tie it, pop it by sitting on it, and go to the end of the team line. First team to pop all of its balloons wins.

BALLOON SMASH

Each person ties a balloon (blown up) around his waist so that the balloon hangs over his back end. Each person also receives a rolled up newspaper. Object is to break everyone else's balloon and keep own from being broken. Newspapers are the only weapon allowed. Last surviving balloon wins.

BALLOON STOMP

Everyone receives a balloon and a piece of string. Each person blows up the balloon and ties it onto his or her ankle with the string. When the game begins, kids try to stomp and pop everyone else's balloon while trying to keep theirs intact. The last person with a balloon wins.

BALLOON SWEEP

In this relay, the players must maneuver a balloon around a goal and back using a broom, sweeping the balloon along the floor. It's much harder than you may think.

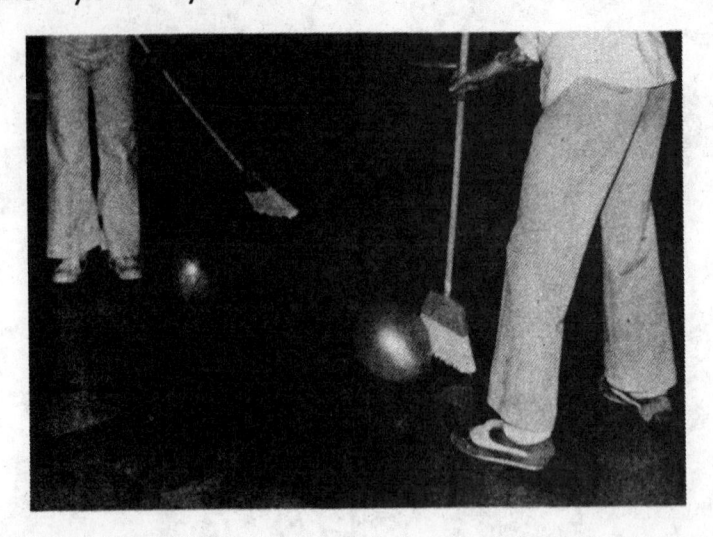

BARNYARD

Give each person a folded piece of paper with the name of an animal written on it. The person is not to say a word or look at the paper. He is to sit down and wait for further instructions. (To insure equal teams assign the same team every 6th person.) After everyone is in and seated, the group is told to look at their team name and when the lights are turned out they are to immediately stand up and make the sound of their animal:

1. Pig
2. Horse
3. Cow
4. Chicken
5. Duck
6. Dog

As soon as they find someone else who is making the same noise, they lock arms and try to find some more of their teammates. When the lights come back on, everyone sits down. The team most "together" wins. For added fun, give *one* guy in the crowd the word "donkey" on his slip of paper. He'll wander around looking for more donkeys without any luck at all.

BIRDIE ON THE PERCH

Have kids pair off and get into two concentric circles. If they are boy-girl couples, then the boys should be in the outside circle and the girls should be in the inside circle.

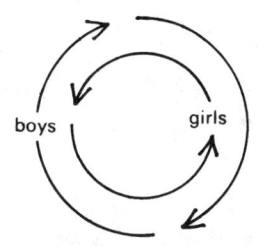

When the whistle blows, the boys circle begins moving clockwise and the girls circle moves counter-clockwise. When the leader yells "Birdie on the Perch!", the boys stop where they are and get down on one knee. The girls must quickly locate their partner and sit on his knee that is extended and put her arms around his neck. The last couple to get into that position is eliminated. The game continues until only one couple remains.

BOTTLE FILL RELAY

Each team appoints one boy to lay down face up with head toward starting line and holding an empty coke bottle on his head. Each team member fills a cup (made of nonbendable material) with water, runs to bottle and pours in water until it is gone. He then runs back and as soon as he crosses the starting line the next contestant runs out with a cup of water and does the same.

BROOM HOCKEY

This game can be played with as many as 30 or as few as 5 per team, but only 5 or 6 are actually on the field at one time from each team. Two teams compete by (at a whistle) running out onto the field, grabbing their brooms and swatting a volleyball placed in the center through the opposite goal. Each team has a "goalie," like in ice-hockey or soccer, who can grab the ball with his hands and throw it back out onto the playing field. If the ball goes out of bounds, referee throws it back in. The ball cannot be touched with hands, or kicked; but only hit with the broom. Score 1 point for each time ball passes between goal markers.

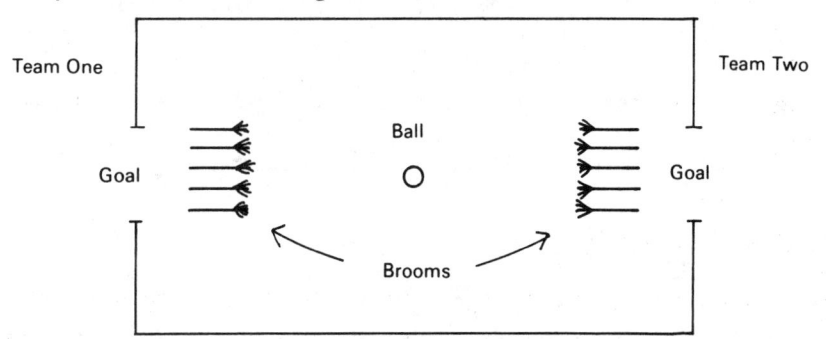

For a team with 30 members, for example, have them number off by sixes, which would give you 6 teams of 5 members each. Let all the "ones" play a 3 minute period, then the "two's," etc.

BROOM TWIST RELAY

Teams line up in normal relay race fashion. At a point some 20 or 30 feet away, a team captain or leader stands and holds a broom. When the game begins, each player runs to his team leader, takes the broom, holds it against his or her chest with the broom end (the bristles) up in the air over his head. Then, looking up at the broom, the player must turn around as fast as possible ten times, while the leader counts the number of turns. Then the player hands the broom back to the leader, runs back to the team and tags the next player who does the same. Players become very dizzy and the results are hilarious.

BUCKET BRIGADE

Each team lines up single file with a bucket of water on one end and an empty bucket on the other. Each team member has a paper cup. The object of the game is to transfer the water from one bucket to the other by pouring the water from cup to cup down the line. First team to get all the water to the empty bucket wins.

BUZZ

This is a good casual game to play indoors. Kids should be seated in a circle. Begin counting around the circle from 1 to 100. Whenever someone comes to a number containing a "7" or a *multiple* of seven, he says "Buzz" instead of that number. For example, it would go: 1,2,3,4,5,6,buzz,8,9,10,11,12,13,buzz,15,16,buzz,18,19,20,buzz,22, etc. You have to stay in rhythm, and if you make a mistake, or pause too long, you are out, or must go to the end of the line.

You can play "FIZZ" which is the same game, except that the number is "5" instead of "7." That makes the game easier for younger kids. To really get the game complicated, play "FIZZ-BUZZ." Combine the two games. It would sound like this: 1,2,3,4,fizz,6,buzz,8,9,fizz,11,12,13,buzz,fizz,16,buzz,18,etc.

CAPTURE THE FLAG

The playing field needs to resemble this:

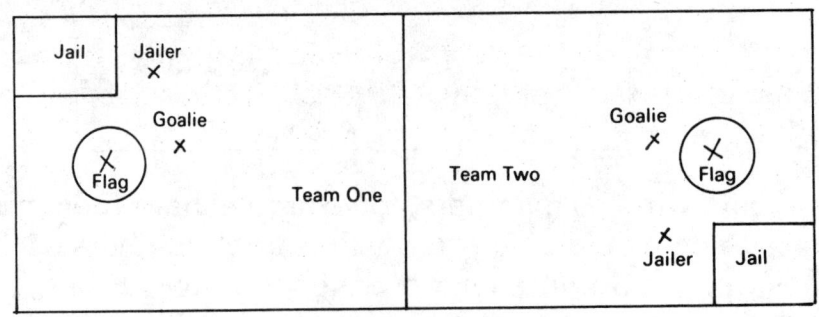

```
+-------+---------------+---------------+-------+
| Jail  | Jailer                                |
|       |   x                                   |
+-------+                                       |
|        Goalie            Goalie               |
|          x                 x                  |
|       (X)                         (X)         |
|       Flag                        Flag        |
|                Team One  Team Two             |
|                                               |
|                                         x     |
|                                       Jailer  |
|                                       +-------+
|                                       | Jail  |
+---------------------------------------+-------+
```

Team 1 is on one side of the field, and Team 2 is on the other side. The idea of the game is to somehow capture the flag, located in the other team's territory, without getting tagged. (Or tackled, clobbered, etc.) Once you cross over the line in the middle of the field, you can be tagged, and set to "jail" which is set up on each team back by the flag. However, if you are in jail, one of your team-mates can free you by getting to the jail without getting tagged, and then he can tag you, which frees you. You both get a free walk back to safety. Each team gets one "goalie" who watches the flag from a distance of about 10 feet away, and also a "jailer," who guards the jail. The idea is to work out some strategy with your team-mates to rush the flag, or in some other way, "capture the flag."

CATERPILLAR RELAY

This is a great game for camps. Have the kids bring their sleeping bags to the meeting, and have races in them, head first. Simply line the teams up, relay style, and the first person in line gets in the sleeping bag, head first, and races to a certain point and back. Of course, he cannot see where he is going, so the team has to shout out directions to him. Each person on the team must do this, and the first team finished is the winner. If you prefer, you can have the kids crawl in their sleeping bags (like a caterpillar) which is slower, but safer.

CHARIOT RACES

This game is best in a gymnasium, or anywhere there is a nice slick floor. Set up a circular "track" and have boys (horses) pull girls (charioteers) on blankets (chariots). There should be two guys pulling and one girl riding. Make sure she is prepared to hold on tightly, as they normally are thrown off the blanket going around curves unless the team works together to prevent that. First team to complete three laps is the winner.

CHARIOT RACE RELAY

Each team chooses sets of two boys and one girl. The number of these sets depends on the size of the teams involved. The two boys face each other and lock their arms, right with right, and left with left. That way the boys' arms are criss-crossed. The girl sits up on the boys' arms, and the boys then race around a goal and back. The next set of players get ready and leave as soon as the previous set returns.

CLUMPS

This game can be used for as many as 1000. Everyone crowds to the center with their arms at their sides. They are instructed to keep moving, but crowd toward the center. They must keep their arms at their sides. The leader blows a whistle or fog horn to stop all movement, and immediately yells out a number. If the number is 4, for instance, everyone must get into groups of 4, lock arms, and sit down. Leaders then eliminate all those not in groups of 4. This process is repeated, with different numbers each time, until all have been eliminated.

COMPARISON SCAVENGER HUNT

This is a good game for camps and outdoor activities. Instead of having a "normal" scavenger hunt, where everybody goes out and brings back specific items on a list, have groups go out and bring back things like:
1. The biggest piece of wood they can find
2. The oldest nickel
3. The smelliest sock
4. The heaviest rock
5. The most worn out shoe (or tire)
6. The rustiest tin-can
7. The ugliest picture
8. The biggest leaf
9. The largest book

Have the kids bring back all the stuff and then one at a time bring each item up for comparison. The group with the "biggest," "oldest," etc. on each team gets points awarded for each item. Arrange for a panel of "judges" who inspect each item and choose the winners.

CROSSWORD PEOPLE

Divide the group into teams of equal size. (12 to 24 on a team.) Prepare ahead of time sets of letters of the alphabet on 12"x12" cards that each team member hangs around his neck. Each team should have identical sets of letters, consisting of frequently used vowels and consonants, plus two of three rarely used letters such as Q, X, or Z. At a signal each team tries to form a "crossword" puzzle, using as many of the team as possible, within a given time limit. Each team should have a captain who directs his team and keeps order. For example, using the letters PGOFYECA JAXTIIUM, a team could line up this way:

```
    JUMPING
       I   O
      TAX  O
          CAFE
           Y
```

Award points for the team using the most of its team, the longest word, the most words, etc. Another idea would be to assign point value to each letter and add points up like if you were playing the game "Scrabble."

"DO IT ON PAPER" SHUFFLE

This is a relay game in which each person is given two pieces of paper (newspaper works fine) and they go between two points stepping only on paper. They step on the paper in front of them, then turn around and pick up the one behind them, and place it in front of them, step on it, and turn around and pick up the paper behind them, put it in front of them, step on it, and so on.

DRIVING THE PIGS TO MARKET

The teams are lined up behind the starting line. Give the first player a three foot stick, yardstick, or broom handle, and a "pig" in the form of a coke bottle or egg. At the signal "go" the first player drives the pig to the goal and back by pushing with wands. The second player does the same until all have run.

EARTH, AIR, FIRE, WATER

Group forms a circle, with the odd man in the center, who throws a ball (or any object) to a person in the circle, and quickly says either "earth," "air," "fire," or "water," and then counts to ten rapidly. (The element of surprise is important here.) The person who receives the ball must, before the odd man finishes his count, respond in one of the following ways: for earth—an animal that lives on the earth (dry land), for air—an animal that flies, for water—an animal that lives in the water, and for fire—he says nothing. If a person responds incorrectly, he takes the odd man's place. You cannot duplicate an answer already given. Each answer must be an "original."

EGG AND ARMPIT RELAY

Half of the team lines up on each side of the room. First person races to the other side with a spoon in his mouth and an egg on it. The team mate on the other side takes the egg and puts it in his armpit and runs back across the room. He must drop the egg from his armpit onto the next person's spoon.

EGG AND SPOON RELAY

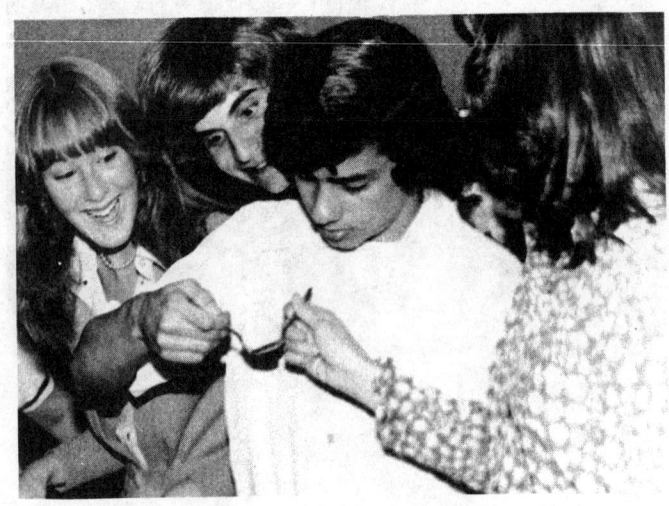

Each player on the team gets a spoon. The teams line up and a dozen eggs are placed on one end of the line. The players must then pass the eggs down the line using the spoons only. You are not allowed to touch the eggs with your hands, except for the first player who puts the egg on his spoon and starts it down the line. The winning team is the one who gets the most eggs down the line (unbroken) in the fastest time.

EGG ROLL

In this relay, contestants roll a raw egg along an obstacle course with their noses. If the egg breaks, the player must start over with a fresh egg.

ESKINOSE

Teams line up, alternating by sex, boy-girl-boy-girl, etc. One person on the end of each line gets a lipstick smear on the end of his (or her) nose. The idea is to see how far down the line you can pass the lipstick smear by rubbing noses. The team that can get it the farthest, or the team that can get it the farthest in the time limit (30 seconds, for example), is the winner. A good prize might be "Eskimo Pies."

EXCEDRIN WAMP

Have each boy (four to six—or as many as 100 to 300) put a paper bag loosely over his head down to his ears. Each boy has a rolled newspaper. The object is to knock the other guy's hat off without losing one's own. No one is allowed to hold their hat on.

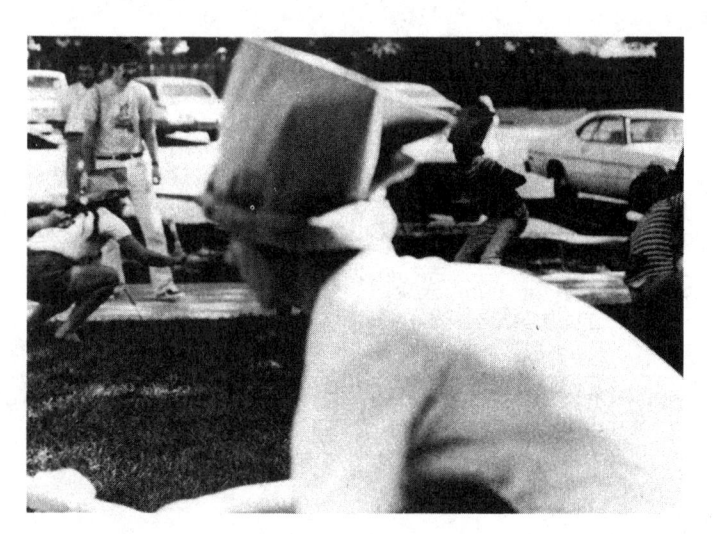

EYE SPY

As a mixer, everyone gets four pieces of paper and each is to list everyone in the room according to color of eyes. (blue, green, brown, grey) First one to finish wins. (Contributed by Jerry Summers, Corpus Christi, Texas.)

FAN THE BALLOON

Each team gets a balloon and a fan (which can be anything such as a record album cover). On the signal, each player on the team must fan the balloon, without touching it, around a goal and back. It also cannot touch the floor.

FLAMINGO FOOTBALL

Announce that you are going to play "tackle football, boys against the girls!" The guys usually get pretty charged up about that idea. Then announce that the rules are the same as regular tackle football, except for one thing. The boys must hold one foot up off the ground with one hand at all times. They must run, pass, hike, catch and even kick on one foot. The girls usually clobber the guys with this one.

FOOTBALL RELAY

This is a good relay race for couples. Each couple must race to a goal and back with a football wedged between them, chin to chin, back to back, and lastly side to side. In other words, each couple races three times. If the ball is dropped, the couple must start over on that particular lap.

FOREHEAD RACE

This relay is for couples on a team. Each couple races to a point and back carrying a grapefruit or balloon between their foreheads. If it is dropped, they must start over.

FRECKLE CLUMPS

As everyone is entering the playing area, each person receives a different number of freckles on their face (with a felt tip pen or "magic marker"). Ten kids get one freckle, ten kids get two, ten kids get three, etc. After everyone is in, blow the whistle to start the game. The kids must find out how many freckles they have on their face and then locate all the other kids that have the same amount of freckles as they do. The winner is the first group of ten to locate each other and sit down on the floor. The last to do so is the loser. Now that your teams are all divided up, you can play team games or relays.

FURNITURE SMASH

Give each team an old piece of furniture, such as a chair, table, bookshelf, etc., that either you get donated, or you pick up at the city dump. The idea is to see who can bust it up and pass the whole thing through a small hole that you cut out of a piece of plywood, or else put the entire smashed up item into a small cardboard box and close the lid.

GIANT JIGSAW PUZZLE

Obtain an outdoor billboard sign from a sign company (they come rolled up and easy to carry), and cut it into a giant jigsaw puzzle. Use it as a game to see which team can put it together first.

GIANT PUSH BALL

It is possible to purchase a "giant push ball" from various sporting goods stores or sporting goods supply houses which is approximately six feet in diameter and weighs close to 100 pounds. It is great for camps and other special activities. Normally the ball is covered with canvas, and is guaranteed for life. A typical push ball game is as follows: Teams line up on either side of an open field. The ball is placed in the middle. On a signal, the two teams (which may consist of any number) try to push the ball through their team's goal on one end of the field. Four teams may play, and have goals on all four sides of the field. The goal can be the entire length of the side of the field. It is really a wild game. For best results, the ball should be pushed upward and over the heads of opposing players.

GRAPEFRUIT PASS

This is a good co-ed relay game. Teams line up boy-girl-boy-girl, etc. A grapefruit is started at one end of the line and must be passed down the line under the chins of the players. No hands are allowed. If the grapefruit is dropped, it must be started at the front of the line again.

HAPPY BIRTHDAY RACE

Divide the group into teams. On a signal, each team must line up according to their date of birth, with the youngest person on the end of the line, and the oldest on the other. Any team out of order after the time limit (or the last team to get in the correct order) loses.

HIDE THE COUNSELOR

This is another good "camp" game. It is merely a game of "hide and seek for big boys and girls." . . . Make the counselors worth points for team competition. Give one special counselor an extra high point value for variety's sake. This could possibly be the camp director. All the counselors then go out and hide, and then the kids are turned loose to find them within a given time limit.
Some sample rules:

1. Counselors get 15 minutes to hide
2. Kids get 15 minutes to search

3. Kids must "tag" counselors to catch them
4. No hiding inside buildings
5. When time is up, remaining counselors come out "free."

For variation, call it a "Dogie Hunt" or a "Manhunt" or an "Elephant Hunt," etc. Also try giving each kid a water balloon, and in order for him to "catch" a counselor, he must hit him with his water balloon.

HULA HOOP PACK

Each team tries to see how many kids they can get inside a hula hoop. Naturally it is best to have your larger kids doing the packing, with the smaller kids getting packed in. If a genuine "hula hoop" is not available, then any strong hoop will work, or a thick rope tied into a circle will work also. Note: If your kids like to pack themselves into things, try packing a phone booth, or a Volkswagen, or a bathtub, or a tractor tire, or anything else you can think of.

HUMAN LAWN MOWERS

This is a good game when you are meeting at someone's home where there is a big back yard, or when you are at a park. Divide into teams and give each person a pair of blunt children's scissors. Each team has a container and the kids must cut the grass with the scissors and fill their team's container with grass. No pulling of the grass by hand is allowed. You must use the scissors. At the end of the time limit (5 to 10 minutes), the team with the most grass wins.

HUMAN WHEELBARROW

This is a relay game in which the boys must walk on their hands while their feet are being held by their partner, boy or girl. Contestants must maneuver through an obstacle course of some kind.

HUNTERS AND HOUNDS

Kids pair off, one being the "hunter" and the other being the "hound." The hunters each get a shoebox (or similar box) and the hounds try to go out and find (for the hunters) peanuts which have been hidden beforehand around the room. When a hound finds a peanut, he cannot touch it, but begins to howl, and his corresponding hunter comes and retrieves the peanut. When two or more hounds find the same peanut, each howls and the hunter who gets there first gets the nut. All hunters wait in a "lodge," a circle or specified area where they wait for their hounds to howl. (Contributed by Jerry Summers, Corpus Christi, Texas.)

IN AND OUT RACE

This is a good game for a "water carnival," or anywhere there is water and boats. Several canoes or rowboats are required. Divide into several teams of five members each. Put each team in a separate rowboat and line the rowboats up evenly in a racing formation. Set up a finish line 50 yards down the course. At the signal, each boat team is to propel themselves as well as possible using only their hands. (Oars are not allowed in the boat.) As the race progresses, the leader is to blow his whistle. Whenever the whistle is blown, all members of each team are to leap out of their boat into the water, climb back into the boat, wait until all members are in the boat, and then paddle on. Leaders are encouraged to blow their whistles often. After several times of "in and out," the boats swamp, and the race becomes a real test of nautical skill.

INDOOR SCAVENGER HUNT

Divide the group into teams. Each team gets into one corner of the room with you in the middle. Each team appoints a "runner" who runs items from the team to you. You call out various items that might be in the group, and each team tries to locate that item among team members, then gives it to the runner, and he then runs it to you. The first team to produce the named item wins 100 points, and after 20 or so items, the team with the most points wins. Make sure that the runners all are running approximately the same distance. Some sample items that you can call out:

A white comb	A turquoise ring or bracelet
A red sock	The smelliest sock you can find
A 1969 penny	(judge to decide the winner)
A student body card	A stick of gum
An eyelash curler	A Theater ticket
A white T-shirt	Picture of your mother
A shoestring (without the shoe)	A Blue sweater

Four belts all tied together
Dark glasses
Picture of a rock star
A twenty dollar bill
Some beef jerky
Denture adhesive
A hat

Toenail clippers
A book of matches
A Cowboy boot
Forty six cents exactly
A Handkerchief
A Timex watch
A book with no pictures

INDOOR SKIING

Make four pair of skis, similar to the diagram below. They should be about five feet long, and made of ¾ inch pine boards. Drill holes one inch from each side at 1,2,3, and 4 feet intervals. Put string (or rope) through each pair of holes. The players' feet fit under these loops. Each team then races around a goal on a pair of these "skis."

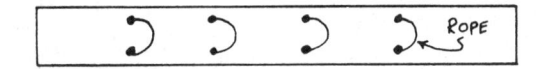

INDOOR OLYMPICS

Below are several simple games that can be used to conduct an "Indoor Olympics." With a little creativity, you can add many more similar games to the list for a very exciting time.

DISCUS THROW: Paper plates are thrown for distance. Plates must be held like a discus. Each contestant takes two hops and a step, then throws the plate as far as he can.

HAMMER THROW: Each contestant throws an inflated paper sack tied onto a 30-inch piece of string. Holding the loose end of the string, each contestant swings the sack around his head several times before throwing for distance.

JAVELIN THROW: Contestants throw toothpicks like javelins. With the throwing arm back, and the other arm out in front for balance, each contestant takes three running steps and throws the toothpick as far as possible. Knitting needles can also be used.

INNER-TUBE OLYMPICS

This is a good snow sport. (Obviously usable only during the winter months.) All you need is a good slope covered with snow, and inner tubes. Either make competition individual or by teams. You (the leader) are the only judge and commentator. The events are: Men and Women's Singles, Men and Women's Doubles, Mixed Doubles, Stunt Riding. Slalom, etc. You award points for **distance rode** and **form**. Poor form criteria: wiping-out, turning the inner-tube while riding it down the hill, closing eyes, etc. Stunt riding is based on originality and distance.

INNER TUBE RELAY

Each team chooses ten couples (or as many as you have). The couples should be of the same sex, rather than boy-girl couples. Each team then lines up in different corners of the room, if that arrangement is possible. Inner tubes (one for each team) are placed in the center of the room. Each couple must run to the inner tube, and squeeze through the tube together, starting with the tube over their heads, and working it down. The first team to have all ten couples finish wins. Inner tubes should be regular auto tire size, and not super small, or very large.

INNER TUBE SOCCER

This is a game of soccer, using the usual rules of the game, only substituting an inner-tube (automobile tire tube) for a normal soccer-style kickball. It really gives the game a new dimension. The tube should lie flat, and the playing surface should be relatively flat and smooth. (Contributed by Jerry Summers, Corpus Christi, Texas)

JOHN – JOHN

This can be used for groups up to 500. Form a circle using everyone. Selected leaders start the game by running to person of opposite sex and yelling, "What's your name?" The person replies, "Linda." The leader looks behind himself and yells, "Linda – Linda . . . Linda – Linda – Linda" while doing a little dance similar to Mexican Hat Dance. The person (Linda in this case) falls in behind the leader, putting her hands on his waist, and together they run to the opposite side of the circle. This time they both do the above together. After they finish the little dance, Linda makes an about face. The leader does the same and grabs on to Linda's waist. The new person grabs on to the previous leader's waist. Now all three proceed to the opposite side of the circle with Linda leading. She would go to a boy. Each chain continues to get longer until everyone is chosen. There would be many chains and the object would be to keep from getting hit by the other chains.

KILL THE UMPIRE

Two people are placed in the center of the room and are blindfolded. One is the Umpire, one is the batter. The "umpire" gets a whistle, the "batter" gets a rolled up newspaper. Every 5 seconds, the umpire must blow the whistle, and the batter tries to hit him with the newspaper. After several people have played, (give each 2 players one or two minutes maximum), secretly remove one of the players blindfolds. (Contributed by Jerry Summers, Corpus Christi, Texas)

KING OF THE CIRCLE

Mark off a big circle (10 feet or so in diameter) and put about a dozen guys into it. At a signal each guy tries to throw everybody else out of the circle, and try to stay in themselves. Last guy to stay in, wins.

KING OF THE GOATS

Choose a "Goat" from the group or one from each team and have them removed while the groups are given instruction. One group, "the crowd" is instructed to stand on the sidelines and shout instructions to the goat while the other group is told to form a circle holding hands. The goat is to be put in the center of the circle blindfolded. On signal the goat is to start chasing the circle and the circle is to move as a whole to avoid being caught. When the goat is ready to start the circle group is instructed in his presence, to move silently and to make no sound and that the goat is to listen to the sideline crowd for his instructions as to which direction to go to catch the circle. As soon as the start signal is given the crowd starts to shout instructions to the goat: Go to the right, the right, now go back, go back, straight ahead, etc. The minute the game gets under way, the Circle team, which had been instructed before the goat arrived, to immediately disband and join the crowd leaving the goat an empty field. Let it run for a short time or until the goat guesses what is going on. (Contributed by Larry Lyon, Fort Lauderdale, Florida)

KING OF THE MOUNTAIN

Divide up into teams (schools, classes, etc.) and give each team a flag that they try to plant on top of a mountain top. Of course, this must be done somewhere like at a camp where there is a mountain to climb. Award points for first, second, third, etc. places, plus points for just getting to the top among the first 10 or so kids.

KLEENEX BLOW

Have the group get into teams. Each team then receives a Kleenex (or any other brand) tissue and they must keep the tissue in the air by blowing, and without touching it. Time each team one at a time, and the team that is able to keep the tissue up in the air the longest is the winner.

LEMON PASS

In this relay, teams pass a lemon down the line using their bare feet only. The lemon is held between both feet cupped in the arches of the feet, and the players must lie on their backs. The first team to get the lemon passed all the way down the line wins.

LIFESAVER RELAY

Divide the group into two lines and give each player a toothpick which he will place in his mouth. The leader will place a lifesaver on the toothpick of the players at the head of each line. It is then passed from toothpick to toothpick until it reaches the end of the line. If it is dropped before it reaches the end of the line, it must be started all over again at the beginning of the line. The winning team is the one whose lifesaver reaches the end of the line first.

LINE PULL

Divide the group into two equal teams. The teams then face each other, by lining up on two sides of a line drawn on the floor. The object of the game is to pull the other team onto your side of the line. You cannot move behind your side of the line farther than three feet, and you must try to reach out and grab somebody on the other side of the line without stepping over the line. Once you are over the line, you are automatically a member of that team and then you must try to help pull the team you were once on over. At the end of the time period, the team with the largest number wins.

MAD ADS

Each team receives a magazine (same one for all teams) and appoints a "runner." The leader then calls out a description of an ad somewhere in the magazine. The first team to tear the ad out of the magazine, give it to the runner, and have the runner give it to the leader, wins. The team with the most "wins" is the victor.

MATCHBOX RACE

This is a relay game in which kids pass a matchbox cover (small wooden type match) down a row of kids from nose to nose without using hands.

MINDREADING GAMES

The following "mindreading" games are all basically alike. There are at least two people who are "clued in" and know how the game is played while the rest of the group is left in the dark. The idea is to try and guess the "code" that the mindreader and his clued-in partner is using to perform the trick involved. As soon as someone in the audience thinks they have the "code" figured out, then allow them to try it and see if they can do it. Keep going until most of the group has finally caught on or until you decide to reveal the code.

"BLACK MAGIC"
While mindreader is out of the room, the audience picks any object. The mindreader returns and the leader points to many different objects, and when he points to the chosen one, it is correctly identified by the mindreader. CODE: The chosen object is pointed to immediately **after** an object that is black has been pointed to.

"BOOK MAGIC"
Several books are placed in a row. One of them is chosen for the mindreader to guess when he returns to the room. The leader points to several books (apparently at random) and when he points to the correct book, the mindreader identifies it. CODE: The chosen book follows any book pointed to that is on the end of the row.

"CAR"
While "mindreader" is out of the room, the crowd picks an object. The mindreader returns and is shown three objects. (One of the three is the correct one.) He correctly picks the chosen object. CODE: The leader calls the mindreader into the room by saying statements that begin with either the letters "C," "A," or "R." (Such as "Come in," "All right," or "Ready") "C" indicates the first object shown, "A" the second, and "R" is the third object. So, when the mindreader is brought into the room, he knows automatically which object it will be.

"THE NINE MAGS"
Nine magazines are placed on the floor in 3 rows of 3. The mindreader leaves the room, and the crowd picks a magazine for the mindreader to identify when he returns. When he does return, the leader, using a pointer of some kind, touches various books in a random order, and when he touches the correct book, it is properly guessed. CODE: The leader touches the very first magazine he points to in one of nine possible places:

1	2	3
4	5	6
7	8	9

Where the leader puts his pointer on the very first book he points to (only), determines where the location of the selected book is in the three rows of three. After pointing to the first book, the leader then can point to as many other books as he wants before pointing to the right one, as the mindreader already knows which book it is.

"RED, WHITE AND BLUE"
This is just like "Black Magic," only it is more confusing, and almost impossible to figure out if you don't know how it's done, and are watching it being performed. The first time the mindreader tries to guess the chosen object, it immediately follows a red object. The next time, a white object, and the third time, a blue object. It just rotates, red-white-blue, etc.

MONOCLE RELAY

This is a relay game, in which the teams line up single file, and the first person in each line places a quarter held over one eye, monocle style, and runs to a given point and back. No hands are allowed after the quarter is in place. If a player drops the quarter, he must come back and start over. The first team to finish is the winner.

MY SHIP SAILS

Have everyone sit around on the floor (or in chairs) and the leader begins the game by taking a towel with a knot in it, or a ball, and says, "My ship sails with . . . (and names something that begins with his initials)." For example, if his name is John Doe, he would say, "My ship sails with juicy donuts, (or jumping ducks, jolly doctors, etc.)." He then throws the towel or ball to another player in the room (who may not know how to play) and he too must say "My ship sails with . . . (?)" If he knows how to play he will say something that begins with his initials. If he doesn't know how to play, he will probably say something that does not begin with his initials, and he must STAND UP. He remains standing until he "catches on" and somebody throws the towel to him and he gets another try. When he gets it right, he gets to sit down. The idea of this game is to see how long it takes people to catch on to what their ship sails with. To start the game, at least 2 or 3 people need to know how to play. You explain at the beginning that not everybody's ship sails with the same thing, and the object is to discover by listening to those who know what their ship sails with, what the secret is.

NEEDLE IN THE HAYSTACK

In a big pile of hay, hide a bunch of large knitting needles, using different colored needles. Make the colors different values, either in points or in money, making the lighter (harder to find) colors more valuable. Turn the kids loose, telling them to throw the hay up in the air for best results. They then bring the needles as they find them to the leader, who announces to the remainder of the kids how many needles are left.

NO-CAN-SEE RELAY

Place two chairs 50 feet apart and place six cans of different sizes on the floor between the chairs. Two players are assigned one of the two chairs as a goal and are blindfolded. The object is for each player to place three cans, one at a time, under his chair. He can steal them from the opponent, or if he runs into the other player, may take his can if he hits it with his hand. Be sure to allow a time limit. The one with the most cans wins.

PAPER AIRPLANE DERBY

Let everybody come up with their own paper airplane, made out of anything that they want, so long as it is paper. Give awards for the best designed airplane, the farthest flight, and the plane that stays in the air the longest. Kids may use paint, glue, and paper, but may not use wire, wood, or metals.

PIKE'S PEAK

Divide the group in half. Each team chooses a captain. Both captains are then stranded on "Pike's Peak" which is located 200-300 yards from "Pike's Dam" (water source). Each captain is holding an empty gallon container. Each team member is given a small Dixie Cup. The object is to fill the cup with water at Pike's Dam (the only water source allowed) and to fill the captain's container. The first team to have a completely full container wins. The object is to stop the other team before they get to the captain by spilling their water, or throwing water all over them.

Rules:
1. Boys can get boys, but boys cannot get girls. (They can run, but no offense.)
2. Girls can get both guys and girls.
3. Within two feet of the captain is a "free zone" and no combat can take place there.
4. It's best to have neutral people at the dam to fill the cups and have each team fill at opposite ends of the water source.
5. Distinguish teams with colored tape on their foreheads. (Or any marking device.)

PILLOW CASE RACE

In this relay, each participant races with both feet in a pillow case. He must hop to a goal and back without stepping out of the pillow case or ripping the pillow case.

PIN THE DONKEY ON THE TAIL

If you can get a live donkey (they are really not that hard to find), here is a variation of an old game. Hang a "tail," which can be a girl's fall or even a piece of old thick rope or something, on a fence, or a bale of hay, etc., and then put the donkey about 30 feet away.

Have a group of about 6 guys try to get the donkey's rear end up against the tail for time. The donkey hates to move in reverse, and usually will refuse to go anywhere, and provides a lot of laughs, but be careful that the guys are instructed to stay away from the donkey's hind feet.

POTATO RACE

Teams line up and each player must push the potato along the floor to a goal and back using their noses only. No hands are allowed.

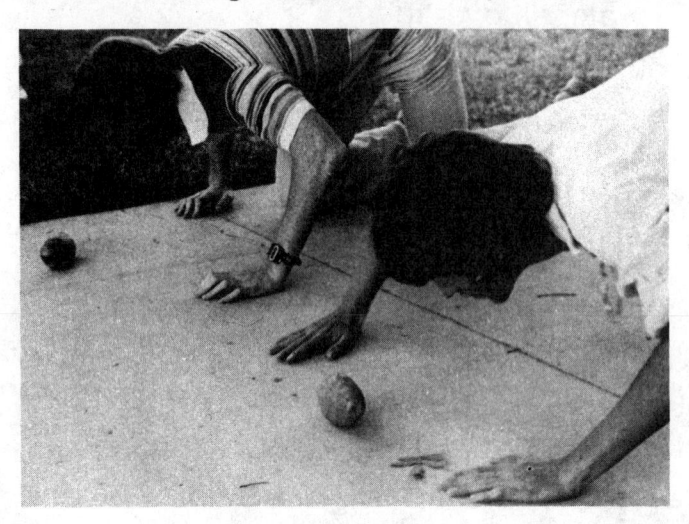

RHYTHM

Everyone in the room numbers off in a circle (1,2,3,4,etc.) with the #1 guy in the end chair. The "rhythm" is begun by the #1 guy and everyone joins in by first slapping thighs, clapping hands, then snapping right hand fingers, then snapping left hand fingers in a continuous 1-2-3-4-1-2-3-4-1-2-3-4, etc. motion at a moderately slow speed. (It may speed up after everyone learns how to play.) The real action begins when the #1 guy, on the first snap of the fingers, calls out his own number, and on the second snap of the fingers, calls out somebody elses number. For example, it might sound something like this: (slap) (clap) "ONE, SIX!", and then the number six guy (as an example) might go: (slap) (clap) "SIX, TEN!", and then the number ten guy would do the same thing, calling out someone elses number on the second finger snap, and so on. If anyone misses, they go to the end of the numbered progression, and everybody who was after him before moves up one number. The object is to eventually arrive at the number one chair.

SACK RACE

This is an old game that is always successful with nearly every age group. Obtain a number of burlap bags (potato sacks) and divide the group into teams. The teams line up, and the first player in each line gets into the sack, feet first, and holds the sack up while hopping around a goal and back. On completion, the next player gets the sack, does the same thing, and the first team to finish is the winner.

SHOE KICK

Have guys take off one shoe, and hang it off the end of their foot. The idea is to see who can "kick" their shoe the farthest. You will be surprised to see how many guys wind up kicking them over their heads, behind them, or straight up in the air.

SHOE SCRAMBLE

Everyone removes their shoes and places them into one big pile. Divide the girls into two teams, and then they must run to the pile of shoes and locate one pair of boy's shoes. (Try to make sure that there are the same number of boys playing this game as girls.) Each girl must then find the owner of the pair of shoes she got off the pile. That boy then becomes that girl's partner and he must then go to the pile and find her shoes from her description of them. The first team to get their shoes on wins.

SHOE SHUCKING RACE

Divide into groups of six (girls must wear pants to play). Each team member must lie on his back with his feet in the air, meeting in the center of the circle. A container of water (dishpan) is placed on the elevated feet. The object is for each member to remove his shoes without spilling his water. The team to win is the one with the most shoes off at the three minute time limit.

SHOULDER SHOVE

Everyone puts their left arms behind their backs, and grab their ankles with their right hands. In this bent over position, they hop around or walk around and try to knock the other players off balance. Anyone who falls down is out of the game. The last player to remain in is the winner. This is best as a ''guys only'' game. Elbowing and lowering of the shoulders is not allowed.

SNOWFIGHT

Two teams are separated by a row of chairs and given a six foot stack of newspaper. They are then given one minute to wad the paper up. When the signal is given, each team then attempts to throw the most paper on the other team's side by the time limit. Each round (usually about 4 rounds per night) is separated by a 30 second break to find everyone who might be buried in the mountain of paper. Team with most paper on their side loses, however, there is always such a mess that a tie is declared. **Caution:** The only way to stop the throwing between rounds is to give the last person who throws something a good penalty (pie in the face, etc.)

SNOW SCULPTURING

This game is great for winter camps and whenever snow is on the ground. Divide the group into teams, and have each group find a spot where the snow is good and thick, and they must "sculpture" anything they want within a given time limit. Encourage them to be as creative as possible. Traditional "snowmen" are not allowed. Sample "sculptures" might include: Cars, famous personalities, buildings, cartoon characters, animals, Santa and his reindeer, etc. Judge to determine the most creative, best job, and degree of difficulty.

SPOON RELAY

Divide the group into two lines, with a spoon in each player's mouth. The leader will place a marble in the spoon of each of the players at the head of the line and they will pass it from spoon to spoon until it reaches the end of the line. The group who reaches the end of their line first will be the winner. If the marble is dropped on its way to the end of the line, it must be started all over again.

SQUATTERS SMASH

This is a good rough game for guys and any number can play. The players squat down on their heels and cross their arms. The object of the game is to hop or walk around in that squatting position and try to knock the other players over. A player is out of the game if he is knocked over. The last person to remain in the game is the winner.

STREETS AND ALLEYS

One person is "it" and chases another person through a maze of people formed in this manner:

```
O   O   O   O
O   O   O   O
O   O   O   O
O   O   O   O
O   O   O   O
```

Everyone in the maze is facing in one direction with their hands joined, forming "alleys." When "streets" is called, all do a right face and grasp hands once more. The person who is "it" tries to catch the runner, and cannot cross the joined hands. When "alleys" is called, everyone in the maze assumes its original position, etc.

STRIPPER RELAY

This is a great game for swimming parties and "water carnivals." Get two or more teams of an equal number of participants. Obtain some baggy clothes (the funnier the better) for each team. Make sure that each team has similar clothing: shirts with buttons, pants with zips, etc., to insure fairness during the relay. Place the clothes in individual team piles about twenty yards from the starting line on a raft or at the end of a pool. At the starting signal, one member of each team swims to the raft or end of the pool, climbs out of the water, puts the clothes on, strips the clothes off, and swims back to his team. He touches the next member of the team who then swims through the same process. First team to finish process wins.

SYMBOL RHYTHM

This is just like "Rhythm" except that instead of numbers, everyone has a "symbol" such as a cough, a whistle, scratching the head, etc. Instead of calling out numbers in rhythm, you give a signal, and everyone needs to be watching pretty closely. Everyone keeps the same signal throughout the game, but you change positions as you move up.

THIMBLE RELAY

The teams form a line, and each player has a straw, which he holds upright in his mouth. The relay is started by placing the thimble on the straw held by the first person in line. It is then passed from player to player by means of the straw. The team which gets the thimble to the end of the line first is the winner.

THREE LEGGED RACE

Two players from each group compete for this event. They stand side by side and the two legs nearest each other are tied together. On the signal go, they race to the goal and back.

TINY TIM RACE

Divide the group into teams. On a signal, each team must line up according to height, with the shortest person on one end and the tallest on the other. The last team to do so, or any team that is out of the proper order is the loser.

TOILET PAPER RELAY

Have each team line up single file and unwind a roll of TP over their heads when the signal is given. Each team continues to unwind the roll up and down the line until it is gone. First team to use up the entire roll wins.

TUG-O-WAR

An old-fashioned tug-o-war never fails to be a winner. Just get a good thick, long rope and put one team on each end of it. Whichever team can pull the other one across the line or into a nice big mud-hole in the middle is the winner. For laughs, put grease all over the rope and see what happens . . .

TWISTER

This game is available at most toy or party stores. It is manufactured by the Milton Bradley Company. It consists of a plastic mat with colored spots on it, and a "spinner" which determines what the players must do. For example, the spinner might say "left hand, yellow," which means that a player must put his left hand on a yellow spot on the mat. The next player spins and might come up with "right foot, red," meaning that he must put his right foot on a red spot, and so on. As the game progresses, the players are forced to become contortionists, and get into some unbelievable positions. The first person to fall over (lose his balance) is the loser.

WADDLE WALK RELAY

Have each team choose four people. Two of the four line up 10 feet from the other two facing them. The object is to balance a cup of water on the head and walk with a balloon filled with air between the knees for the prescribed distance. If either the water or balloon fall, the person must start over. The first team to have all four contestants finish wins.

WADDLE TO THE BOTTLE

In this relay, teams race with players carrying a small coin (penny, dime) between their knees. They must successfully drop the coin into a milk bottle or jar placed 15 or 20 feet away without using their hands. If the coin is dropped along the way, the player must start over.

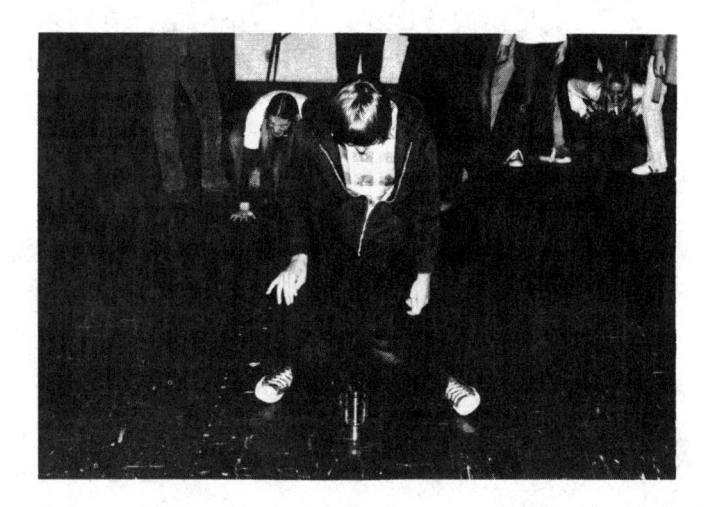

WATER BALLOON BLITZ

Divide into two teams. Give each team 15 minutes to fill balloons (make sure there are plenty of water outlets). When the starting signal is given, everybody unloads balloons until stock is finished. Winner is the driest team. Be sure to announce the meeting before that any participant can wear any protective items he wants (garbage can tops, goggles, etc.). Suggested number of water balloons to give out:

     One team of 50 kids . . . . 200 balloons
     One team of 100 kids . . . . 400 balloons
     One team of 150 kids . . . . 600 balloons
     One team of 200 kids . . . . 800 balloons

WATER BALLOON RELAY

Use as many couples as you want. Each couple races between two points holding a water balloon between their foreheads. Of course, the couples are facing each other and walk sideways. They cannot use their hands to hold the balloon. If the balloon drops, the couple picks it up and keeps going. If it breaks, they are out of the game.

WATER BALLOON SHOT PUT

This is a simple game to see who can toss a water balloon "shot put" style the farthest. To give the players added incentive, the youth leader can stand at a place just out of reach of the shot-putters, and they use him as a target.

WATER BALLOON TOSS

Couples line up facing each other, and are given a water balloon which they toss back and forth at a signal of some sort. Each time they move one step farther apart. Last couple to keep their water balloon in one piece wins.

WATER CARNIVAL

Next time you have a "pool party" or a swim meet at camp, try some of these games:

1. *Walk the Plank*—Tie a long narrow pole onto the diving board so that it extends out over the water. It can be fastened on with good rope. Mark it off at one foot intervals all the way out to the end of the pole. Kids then see who can walk out on it the farthest. The markings on the pole indicate how far each person gets.

2. *Submarine Races*—See who can swim the farthest underwater.

3. *Ugly Dive Contest*—See who can dive the craziest, most unusual dive. Have the non-participants judge.

4. *Cannon-Ball*—See who can make the biggest splash off the board.

5. *Pearl Diving Contest*—Kids dive for money thrown into the pool. The team with the most money wins.

6. *Potato Race*—This is done in shallow water, but can be done in deep water if your kids are good swimmers. Kids carry a potato in a spoon to a goal and back, relay style. If the potato falls off, it must be picked up with the spoon. You cannot touch the potato with your hands.

WELLS FARGO

This game is best at a camp or wherever there is plenty of running room, terrain, trees, and good places to hide. It is also best with more than 50 kids, and can be played with as many as a thousand. It can be a dangerous game, resulting in injuries unless there is strict enforcement of the rules and every safety precaution taken. But the risk is usually worth it, as the game is one of the most exciting camp games ever created.

Divide the entire group into two teams, the Cowboys and the Indians. Indian headbands, war paint, cowboy hats, etc. help to make the game more fun, but are not necessary. In the center of an open field, mark off an 8 by 8 foot area which becomes the "bank." A large garbage can can be used as the bank, if you prefer. You will also need to prepare a number of "bags of gold" that can be potato sacks filled with rocks. They should be light enough that they can be carried by one person, or tossed from one person to another. You will also need a piece of tape for each person. These are stuck on everyone's forehead and become their "scalps." (It is safer, however, to place them on their arms rather than their foreheads.) It is best to get two different colors of tape to distinguish the cowboys from the Indians, but you can simply mark the pieces of tape with X's and O's. Each player must wear their scalp so that it can be easily seen. They can't be hidden under hats, hair, clothing, and the like.

To start the game, the cowboys get the gold and have ten minutes to hide out in the woods or wherever, and at a signal, the Indians are released to try and find them. There are two objectives to the game: (1) To get the gold, or in the cowboys' case, to get the gold into the bank, and (2) to get scalps (tape). The cowboys try to get the gold in the bank, because if they don't, they don't get credit for it. If the Indians can capture it by overpowering the cowboys who have it, it becomes theirs and the cowboys cannot get it back. As a safety measure, boys cannot attack or scalp girls, but girls *can* attack and scalp boys. It is best for kids to travel in groups and work out their strategies. Cowboys may scalp Indians as well as vice-versa. Once you are scalped, you are "dead," and must go to boot hill. You are out of the game.

The bags of gold are worth 1000 points each. Cowboys must get it into the bank or it is worthless to them if they still have it in their possession at the end of the game. The Indians don't have to put it in the bank to collect their points. All they have to do is capture it and stash it someplace until the game is over. The scalps are worth 100 points each. The game can last 30 to 45 minutes or so, and at the end of the game the teams add up their scores, based on how many scalps they have and how many bags of gold they got in the bank or captured. The team with the most points wins.

WHEELBARROW EAT

Divide the group into teams and have everyone on the teams pair off. One partner walks on his hands, with the other partner holding his feet (wheelbarrow style). Each pair has a trail of food items, such as bread, grapes, etc., on the floor, and the partner who is the wheelbarrow must follow the food trail and "eat" his way to the goal. The first team to do so is the winner.

Chapter Three

The "Hot Seat"

The "hot seat," or the "electric chair" as it is sometimes called, is a great youth programming tool, ideal for use as a crowd breaker. Essentially it is an ordinary wooden stool that has been wired with a six-volt lantern battery and a Model-T coil. Its function is to give the person sitting on the "hot seat" a harmless electric shock that usually sends him (or her) leaping off the seat. There are rarely (none that we know of) any side-effects or lasting pain inflicted by the "hot seat," and when it is properly used, it can be a tremendous source of enjoyment for any group of young people. The fun is watching each other's varied (and they *are* varied) responses to the shock. The "hot seat" was developed and widely used in the nationwide network of "Campus Life" clubs and has been used for fun in many other youth programs from coast to coast.

A PHILOSOPHY OF THE "HOT SEAT"

The key to the success of the "hot seat" is in how you use it. If it is not properly managed, it can be a negative factor in your youth programming instead of a positive one. Therefore, the following guidelines are offered:

1. Never use the "hot seat" as a disciplinary tool or for serious revenge or retaliation. It must be used strictly for fun. It is designed to provide humor and positive audience response. It can be very entertaining, but not if it is used for discipline. When it is used for fun, kids will usually look forward to the day when they get chosen to sit on it, simply because everyone likes a good

sport and it is fun to be able to make people laugh. That is not always the case, of course, as some kids will have a fear of the "hot seat" that just won't go away. Avoid selecting those kids to sit on it.

2. Don't put kids on the "hot seat" against their will. If a kid is truly frightened of the potential shock, then try not to select him or her if at all possible. Use kids who are more willing. They are the most fun anyway.

3. Use the "hot seat" sparingly. Only zap two or three kids per meeting. That way the kids will look forward to seeing it again, rather than be tired of it due to over-use.

4. Don't use the "hot seat" with little children, old people (especially the elderly) or kids with potentially dangerous health problems. The "hot seat" is best with junior high through young adult age groups. Although the electric shock itself is harmless (much like the shock you receive on certain days when you slide across a carpeted floor and then touch a doorknob . . .), the emotional shock or a needless fall could result in injuries.

5. Take every precaution to insure safety. Regardless of who is sitting on the "hot seat," always be prepared to catch a person should they fall backward. And *never* use the "hot seat" near the edge of a stage or platform, as the shock could send the person flying over the edge. Keep sharp objects, corners of tables, etc., away from the immediate area where the "hot seat" is being used.

6. Don't zap the same people every time you use the "hot seat." Try to avoid having any one person on the seat more than once or twice a year. There may be exceptions, of course, but generally this is a good rule of thumb.

7. Don't use the "hot seat" every meeting. Once a month is plenty, and may be too often if your group is small. You may find it wise to keep it locked up except for perhaps twice a year, or even once a year at summer camp or a similar activity. Use your own judgment on this, but it is possible that if kids know that the "hot seat" will be at every meeting, they may just decide to stay home, rather than risk the possibility of having to sit on it. Again, use it sparingly for best results.

8. Don't let the kids mess around with it before or after the meeting. It is advisable to disconnect it somehow until you are ready to use it. Otherwise, the kids will be zapping everybody in sight. One suggestion is to have a removable push button chord that simply plugs in and out. You can then keep the push button in your pocket, and the "hot seat" won't work until you plug it in.

9. Be prepared to sit on the "hot seat" yourself. Your time will undoubtedly come. Don't use it at all unless you have a good attitude towards getting zapped yourself. It's really not too bad . . .

HOW TO USE THE "HOT SEAT"

Generally speaking, the "hot seat" is of no value just by itself. You never want to simply pull it out and start shocking people. It's real value is when it is used along with crowd breakers, games and stunts such as those suggested below. There are literally hundreds of different ways to use the "hot seat" and to select volunteers. Here are a few:

1. *Games of Chance.* There are ways to select people to sit on the "hot seat" that are purely based on luck. A good example is the "Hot Potato", bought in most toy stores. You simply wind it up and pass it around the room from person to person. Whoever is holding it when the bell rings inside the potato (it takes about 20 seconds or so) gets to sit on the "hot seat." The tension really mounts as the potato is passed around the group.

2. *Games of Skill.* The most common way to use the "hot seat" is with simple crowd breakers that require a degree of skill. One example: You move your arms up and down in a vertical man-

ner. The kids are instructed to clap their hands (once) every time your hands cross in the middle. Anyone who goofs gets the "hot seat." Everybody has to play. Non-participants can be zapped automatically. By "almost" crossing your hands, kids will clap when they're not supposed to. You watch, and select one person at a time. You will usually have plenty of people who goofed to choose from. Sometimes it is a good idea to have helpers out in the group watching for you to select your "volunteer."

3. *Competitive Events.* Throughout the IDEAS series are quick little games that involve a small number of kids in some sort of humorous competition. The "hot seat" can be a great "motivator" when they know that the loser will be a candidate for "riding the hot seat." An example of this is the "Forty Inch Dash," which is described in the "Crowd Breakers" chapter of this book. The last person to succeed in reaching the marshmallow gets the "hot seat." It is best, however, to avoid always giving the loser of such an event a "penalty" such as this. It is a good idea to emphasize the positive by giving the winner a prize of some kind. Listed below are a few other competitive events in this book that can be used very well with the "hot seat" in the same way as the before-mentioned idea. There are hundreds of others found in other volumes of IDEAS.

>   Canned Laughter
>   Corn Shucking Race
>   Romeo
>   Silly String War
>   Speech Spasm
>   Boob Tube
>   Twister

4. *Hot Seat Games.* There are a number of games that directly involve the use of the "hot seat." Here are three examples:

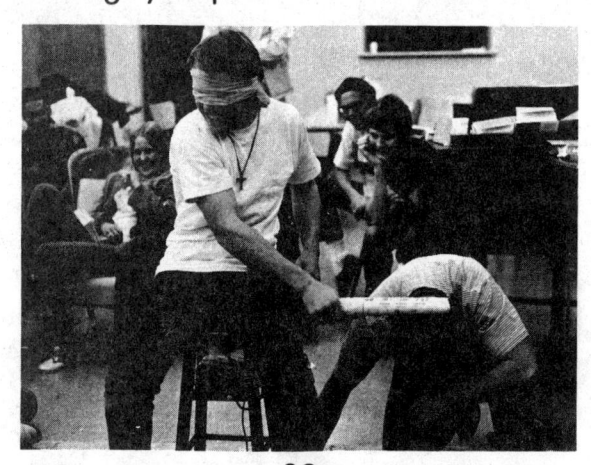

BLIND MAN'S WHOMP: Pick a guy or girl to sit on the "hot seat." Blindfold him and give him a rolled up newspaper in each hand. Another guy is picked from the audience and told to try and get to the "hot seat" button, which is placed directly under the seat. The guy on the "hot seat" tries to hit the button grabbing guy with the newspapers before he gets to the button. If he is hit before he gets to the button, he gets the "hot seat" and the guy who *was* on the seat gets to push the button free.

PUZZLE PANIC: This is a race for time, using the "hot seat." A guy or girl sits on the seat and is given a child's wooden puzzle, consisting of about eight or ten puzzle pieces all mixed up. They have one minute to put the puzzle together or they get "zapped." They have no way of knowing how much time they have left until the minute is up, when you push the button. Although the puzzle will usually be very simple, easily put together by most pre-schoolers, the pressure of putting it together while sitting on the "hot seat," with a deadline of one minute, makes it almost impossible for most high-schoolers.

TALKATHON: Select three or four volunteers from the audience. Tell them that they are to be involved in a "talkathon" that involves acute timing. Each one of them is to be placed on the "hot seat." They are told to speak (on any subject) non-stop for as close to one minute as possible. Each one of them will be timed and the person who speaks the shortest length of time will be penalized by getting "zapped." They are also told that if they *exceed* the one minute time limit while sitting on the "hot seat," they will also be zapped. (You just push the button when the minute is up.) When the volunteer stops talking, he gets off the chair and you announce the time (how long he talked). Have a stopwatch and use tenths of a a second for added suspense. At the conclusion, times are compared and the "loser" gets it in (or on) the seat.

5. *Group Games.* Many games involve team competition, rather than individual competition. It is possible to put the *entire team* that lost on the "hot seat" and zap them ALL AT ONCE. Here's how: Two people sit back to back on the "hot seat," one on the positive side and one on the negative side of the seat. The rest of

the group (any number of kids) get in a circle and hold hands, connecting with the two people who are sitting on the seat. The idea is to have the electrical current flowing all the way around the circle from the positive side to the negative side. Have all the kids hold their clasped hands up in the air to make sure that they are all holding hands, then push the button. They will *all* get it in the hands. It's really a lot of fun. Note: If anyone breaks the connection (doesn't hold hands) before you push the button, it won't work.

6 *Crowd Control.* The "hot seat" is a great way to get everyone seated or quiet in a meeting situation. Just yell out "Last one seated gets the hot seat." It's amazing how fast they cooperate. Again, it's important that you not use the "hot seat" as a disciplinary tool, but only as a fun way to get action.

HOW TO "ZAP" SOMEONE ON THE "HOT SEAT"

Half the fun of using the "hot seat" is in the way you actually do the "zapping." The obvious way to do it is to simply have the selected person sit on the seat while you push the button. However, there are other variations of administering the "hot seat" that add to the excitement or humor of the situation:

1. *The Countdown.* Have the audience count backwards with you from five as loudly as possible. Say to the crowd, "Let's give him the countdown! Five! . . . Four! . . . Three! . . . Two! . . . One! . . . LIFT OFF!" You push the button and the person actually does "lift off."

2. *Countdown Fake.* Same as above, except when the audience reaches zero, you don't push the button. The person on the seat just sits there. You ask him, "Didn't you feel anything? . . . Amazing!" Then push the button.

3. *The Sex Problem.* Have the person who has been chosen for the "hot seat" to sit down on it. Then act as though you just remembered the following announcement and it cannot wait: "SAY, I

forgot to mention that next week our discussion topic will be sex. We need some volunteers to be on a panel, so if you have a serious sex problem, would you please stand up?" You then push the button, and the person on the chair jumps up.

4. *Volunteer Announcement.* This is done the same as the sex problem announcement, except that you ask for volunteers to clean up after the meeting to stand, and then you push the button.

5. *Terminology.* Here are a few things that you can say while using the "hot seat" that adds to the humor:

"This is the original 'bunsen burner.' We brought it along to burn a few bunsens."
"You'll get a real charge out of this!"
"This will give you a real lift!"
"Congratulations. You've won a free Bar-B-Q."
"You've just won a free rump roast!"
"Are you chicken? Well, now you're going to be FRIED chicken!"

6. *The "Anti-Incineration Pass."* This pass entitles bearer to one free escape from the "hot seat." If he is chosen for some reason during a meeting to get zapped, upon presentation of the "Anti-Incineration" pass he doesn't have to sit on the seat, but gets to choose someone else in the group to take his place. Print some of these passes up and give them away as prizes for stunts or give one to people who have just got zapped.

HOW TO BUILD YOUR "HOT SEAT"

You will need to purchase the following items:

1. An Unfinished wooden stool (from a hardward store, or an unfinished furniture store).
2. Model T Coil (available at many automotive supply stores, antique auto suppliers, or antique and junk shops).
3. Push button (called a "momentary switch." Easily obtained at an electrical supply store.)
4. A 6-volt dry cell battery.
5. Various lengths of wire.
6. Two small pieces of screen material.
7. Black electrical tape.

The wiring and construction of the "hot seat" should be done according to the diagram on the next page. Mount the battery and coil on a small platform that you build right under the seat. Fasten everything down securely, as it might fall off when the "hot seat" falls over or gets kicked around.

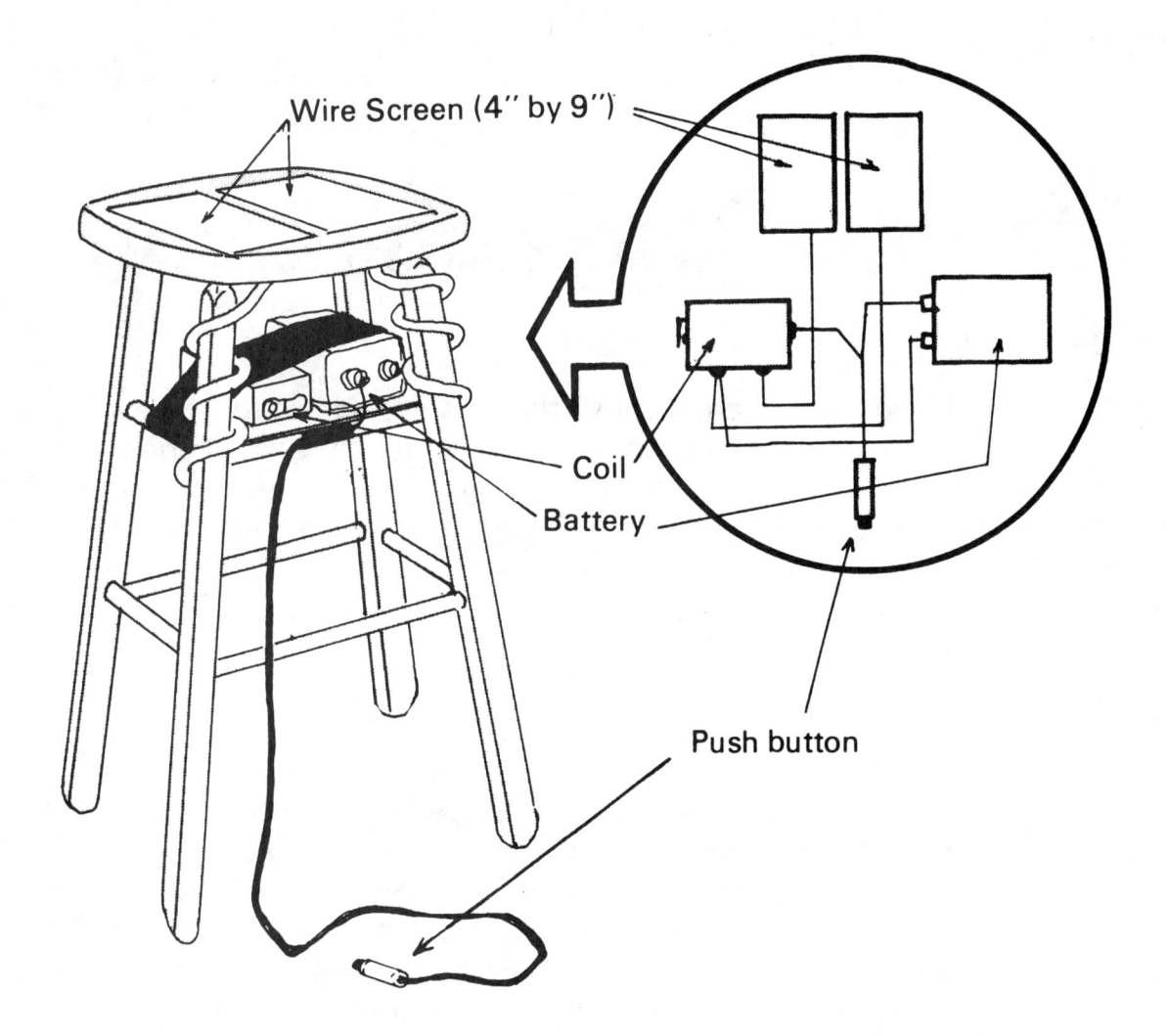

Paint your "hot seat" in bright colors, and make it as attractive as you desire. It is also possible to mount all the electrical parts onto regular chairs (rather than stools), or smaller wooden boxes with the screen on top, to make it more portable or compact.

Warning: Many people have made "hot seats" by using a six-volt transformer (such as the electric train variety) in place of the battery. This use of household electric current is potentially dangerous and should be avoided.

Chapter Four

Creative Communication

COP OUT

Invite a policeman to answer questions from the group. Have each person write out questions on blank paper. (Be sure to tell them *not* to put their name on the paper.) The policeman then reads them back and answers them and discusses the answers with the group. Be sure to set a time limit for each answer like 2 minutes (not including discussion).

DISCUSSION

Objectively, informal discussion is an oral exchange of ideas, facts, and opinions by a group of persons. Subjectively, however, informal discussion is the best way for meaningful communication to occur in a youth group. Discussion can easily be prostituted to force young people to arrive at a pre-arranged conclusion, or to be a forum for the leader's opinions. Care must be taken, therefore, to insure uninhibited and free discussion. The following suggestions will help.

1. The atmosphere must be one of complete freedom. Each participant must be allowed to say whatever he believes without fear of ridicule, embarrassment or correction. Non-participation must also be acceptable. (In other words, refrain from calling on individuals because they are not participating or not interested.)

2. Although the leadership can be shared by the group, in most church situations discussions are led by an adult or older person. In those situations the leader must understand his role as a facilitator. It is his responsibility to help the participants share honestly in an atmosphere of openness. The leader can either be a neutral observer helping only with the mechanics of the discussion, or he can be an equal participant whose opinion and importance is equal with the group. In either case, the leader must be well-prepared with questions and specific goals in mind. (Note: goals do not mean a specific conclusion, rather a specific focus so that a conclusion is reached.)

3. If the leader is going to speak at length about the topic or any aspect of the discussion, it is best to wait until the end and summarize what has been said by the group and then comment. The "wrap-up" or conclusion by the leader should not be used to re-

fute or attack any opinions already expressed. Basically, the "wrap-up" is a positive statement of what the leader believes.

Discussions can be stimulated through many creative techniques. The most common is the question and answer method. Below are some examples for you to use as guidelines in preparing your own discussion. Note that the questions are as objective as possible. (Avoid loading questions, e.g., "Do non-Christians enjoy life, or do they just *think* they do?")

Language
1. What does "Using the Lord's name in vain" mean?
2. What makes a word a swear word?
3. Does Christianity affect the words we use?

Models
Give a piece of paper to each group member. Have them write the name of a person they most respect or would like to emulate.

1. Share with the group the name of your model and the reason you chose him.
2. If you couldn't think of a model, why? Was it because there aren't any worth having? Because you haven't thought about it? Because you have so many? Why?
3. Are there contemporary Christians that you would consider for a model?
4. Do your models affect your life?

Church
1. Describe the ideal church.
2. What would you change in your church, if anything?
3. Do you think churches should be tax exempt?
4. Define an ideal minister.
5. Is it necessary to attend church?
6. What is the purpose of church?

Honesty
1. Try to recall the most recent lie that you have told.
2. Try to imagine a situation where personal dishonesty would be worthwhile.
3. What is the most dishonest act that a person can perform?
4. Name an incident where your friends were dishonest with you.
5. What things do you encounter that make it difficult for you to be honest?

There are many other ways to begin a discussion and you will find a number of them throughout our IDEAS series. Here are some suggestions:

1. *Story/illustration:*
   A fictional or non-fictional illustration which focuses on an issue to be discussed.

2. *Film:*
   Feature length theatre films or short, open-ended discussion films.
3. *Topics:*
   A discussion using only the topic itself as a stimulater (cheating, racism, sexism, etc.).
4. *Case Study:*
   An in-depth case history of a specific person.
5. *Problem-solving:*
   A problem is presented and a solution must be decided on by the group.
6. *Role Plays:*
   Short situations acted out extemporaneously and analyzed.
7. *Simulation Games:*
   Games simulating a real situation in which all members are involved.
8. *Creative Expression:*
   Non-verbal expressions of truth or experience such as painting, sculpture, dance, etc.
9. *Values Clarification:*
   Strategies or exercises aimed at raising value consciousness through conflicting value choices.

GROUPERS

Groupers are short "written discussions" or unfinished sentences such as "I wish I were . . ." that can be used to stimulate discussion. Through Groupers, young people can express and explore their beliefs and goals and as a result discover what their values really are. There are two ways to use Groupers. The first is as follows:

1. Supply each person in the group with pencil and paper (golf pencils and index cards work great).
2. Have each person complete the Grouper (unfinished sentence). The Grouper can be given to the group orally, or you can write it on the blackboard, or have it printed up ahead of time.
3. Emphasize that there are no restrictions on the content of the completed sentences other than that they should be as honest as possible. The emphasis in this exercise is on spontaneous true reflections of each individual and not on the "rightness" or "wrongness" of the responses. No answer is unacceptable. Each person has the right to pass.
4. After everyone has finished completing their Grouper, the cards are collected by the leader and read back individually (they should be folded in half with no name attached).
5. The group can discuss each answer separately, or wait until all the finished Groupers have been read.

6. The leader can then conclude the discussion by reading his own completed sentence (Grouper) and sharing why he responded as he did. Or he may prefer to comment on some of the answers given by the group and introduce some content. (Example: "I was surprised how many of you responded to the statement, 'I fear most . . .' with the words 'being alone.' Surprisingly, loneliness was a common dilemma of many people in the Bible. Let's take a look . . .")

Another way to use Groupers is to vary the above procedure by having each person read back to the group his completed Grouper. This works best if the members of the group know each other well, and if there is an atmosphere of freedom and trust among members of the group. Each person can elaborate on his answer and can answer questions from the group, but reserves the right not to answer any questions as well. Again, no answer is unacceptable and each person has the right to pass.

Below are sample "Groupers." While there are many excellent ones here, don't limit yourself entirely to them. These can be a guide for designing your own Groupers that best suit the topic that you wish to discuss.

1. I fear most . . .
2. I wish I were . . .
3. I wish I were not . . .
4. I wish I had . . .
5. I wish I had not . . .
6. I wish I could . . .
7. If I were the President, I would . . .
8. The President should . . .
9. The happiest day of my life was . . .
10. If I could start this year over, I would . . .
11. My favorite place is . . .
12. My parents should . . .
13. I wish my parents wouldn't . . .
14. What hurts me the most is . . .
15. If I had $25, I would . . .
16. I would like to tell my best friend . . .
17. The worst thing a person could do is . . .
18. What always makes me mad is . . .
19. If I could do anything, and no one else would know, I would . . .
20. I always cry when . . .
21. I always laugh when . . .
22. I hate . . .
23. If I were principal of my school, I would . . .
24. If I had a million dollars, I would . . .
25. If my parents left me alone, I would . . .

26. The most important thing in my life is . . .
27. If I had X-ray vision, I would . . .
28. The hardest thing for me to do is . . .

THE ISLAND AFFAIR

This story is very effective as a means to help young people discover their beliefs and convictions. As they respond and comment on the happenings in the Island Affair, their values will surface in a non-threatening manner.

Use the diagram below while telling the story.

The two circles represent two islands surrounded by shark infested waters. As a result of a shipwreck, only five survivors manage to reach the safety of the islands. Albert is separated from his fiancee, Carla. Carla is stranded on the other island with her mother, Della. Bruno, a young man of about the same age as Albert ends up on Albert's island. The fifth survivor is an older man, Edgar. He is a loner, but is situated on the same island with Carla and Della.

The situation is this: Albert and Carla are deeply in love and engaged to be married. After two months of being separated and yet in sight of each other, they desperately long to be joined. But each passing day makes rescue look more hopeless. Carla becomes despondent. One day while walking around the island, Carla discovers a crude boat hollowed out of an old tree. It looks seaworthy. Then Edgar appears. He has just finished making the boat. Carla explains her longing to reach the other island and Albert and pleads with Edgar to let her have the boat. Edgar refuses saying the boat was made for his escape and not hers. After continued pleading by Carla, Edgar makes a proposal. If Carla will make love to him, he will take her to the other island in his boat. Carla asks for time to consider and runs to find her mother, Della. She explains to her mother that rescue looks hopeless and that if they are to be stranded on an island she should at least be with the one she loves. Della listens with understanding and after much thought gives her advice. "I know you sincerely love Albert and I understand your desire to be with him. But I am afraid the cost is a bit high. It is up to you to do what you want, but my advice would be to wait a bit longer. I'm sure a better solution will come and you will be glad you waited."

Carla considers her mother's advice for a number of days. Finally, she decided to accept Edgar's offer. Carla makes love to Edgar. Edgar keeps his part of the bargain and rows Carla to Albert's island. Albert and Carla embrace and are very happy. But during the day's conversation, Carla recounts for Albert the situation that drove her to strike a bargain with Edgar. She confesses that she made love to Edgar, but only because she loved Albert so much. Albert is deeply hurt. He tries to understand, but after long discussion and thought he tells Carla that although he loves her very much, he could not continue their relationship knowing that she had made love to another man. Carla tries to change Albert's mind, but to no avail.

While this discussion is going on, Bruno is listening from behind some bushes. When Albert leaves, Bruno comes to Carla and explains that he thinks what she did was admirable. He understands that her experience with Edgar was the result of desperation and was an act of love for Albert. Bruno tells Carla that he would readily accept someone who would pay such a high price for their love and he would be willing to care for Carla in spite of what Albert did. Carla accepts.

Provide each person in the group with paper and pencil and have them rank the characters in the story from best to worst. Break up into small groups and have the groups agree on a choice for best person and worst person. Then have a spokesman from each group share with the entire group their choices and the reasons for their choices. Good discussion can follow.

Further discussion can center around the following questions.

CARLA:
1. Was she justified in what she did to be with Albert?
2. Should she have accepted Bruno's proposal?

ALBERT:
1. Should he have accepted Carla?
2. If Albert were a Christian, would he have behaved differently?

DELLA:
1. Was her advice acceptable? If not, what advice would you have given?

EDGAR:
1. Is there any justification for his action?

BRUNO:
1. Why do you think he accepted Carla?
2. Would you have accepted her?

WILL OF GOD

The following questions should be duplicated and given to each member of the group to answer with a "yes" or "no." Then go back and discuss them.

YES   NO
1. Has God ever communicated with you directly?
2. Does God have an absolute moral standard for Man?
3. Is man responsible to God for his actions?
4. Can two people be led by God to do that which is the opposite of the other?
5. Has God already chosen a wife or husband for you?
6. If you make a wrong major decision, can you ever be in God's will?
7. Have you ever consulted the Bible when making a decision and found help?
8. Should God be consulted when selecting a career?
9. Should God be consulted when buying clothes?
10. Should God be consulted when selecting a deodorant?

Chapter Five

Special Events

BIGGER AND BETTER HUNT

The entire group meets at a central location for instructions. The group is divided into small groups of 4 or 5, who go together on foot, in cars, or (if the group is very large) in buses. Each team is given a penny to begin with, and the idea is for the team to go to someone's home in the neighborhood and trade the penny for something "bigger and better". They then take the item that they received in trade for the penny to the next house and attempt to trade that item again for something "bigger and better." The team is not allowed to trade for cash. It has to be an item that the person at each house is willing to give in exchange for whatever the team has at that time. Team members are not allowed to "sweeten the pot" by adding more money to the original penny or any of the items along the way. Each team has one hour (or so), and at the end of the time limit, the teams meet back at the central location and show what they finally ended up with. The group with the "biggest and the best" is the winner. This has been used successfully with many different groups, and some groups have traded for such items as washing machines, watermelons, electric toasters, and all kinds of very usable stuff. The items collected can be used later in a rummage sale, or may be donated to a local service organization. (Contributed by Jerry Summers, Corpus Christi, Texas)

BLOW-OUT

A "Blow-out" is a special event based on tires, or cars. Choose up teams, name them ("The Uniroyals," "The Goodyears," etc.) and play some of these wild games:

1. *Tire Relay.* Roll tires with a person inside it. Race relay style.

2. *Inner Tube Pack.* See how many kids each team can get inside a large tractor tire tube (around the waists).

3. *Scavenger Hunt.* Kids go around the neighborhood and try to bring back old tires or inner tubes.

4. *Tire Change.* Teams race to see which can change a tire on all four wheels of a car (rotate the tires, in other words.)

5. *Dive Through.* Hang a tire from a tree by a rope. Each team races to see which can all dive through the tire in the fastest time. Or, set a time limit like one minute. Each team tries to get as many

kids through the tire in the time limit as possible.

6. *Tire Slalom*. Set up a slalom course and teams roll the tires along the course all at the same time. Turning sharp corners is not easy, and kids running their tires into each other becomes a real problem.

7. *Tire Stack.* If you have enough tires, teams compete to see which can stack a pile of tires one on top of the other the highest.

8. *Tire Eat.* This is like a pie eating contest, only you use "Angel Food Cake" which has a hole in the middle and resembles a tire. Each team chooses one hungry player to compete.

9. *Capture the tube.* Put all the tires and tubes in the middle, with each team's territory marked off around the tubes. On a signal, the players grab the tires and try to get as many as they can into their territory. Once it is in a team's territory, it cannot be captured by any other team.

COME AS YOU WERE PARTY

The theme of this event is babies. Everybody is supposed to come to the party dressed up like a baby. Then try some of these games:

1. *Best Dressed Baby.* Judge for the best costume worn to the party.

2. *Baby Picture Guess.* Everyone brings a baby picture of themselves, and you hang them all up on the wall. Kids then try to

match them up.

3. *Baby Burp.* Select a couple from each team. The boys drink a bottle of pop and try to burp while the girls slap them on the back. Do it one at a time, and judge for the loudest, longest, etc.

4. *Baby Buggy Race.* Get an old baby carriage or stroller for each team. Then have a race, relay style, with each person pushing the carriage around a goal and back with one of their teammates riding on it.

5. *Bottle Drinking Contest.* Give guys a baby bottle full of warm milk. The first to finish it wins.

6. *Diaper Change.* Give girls large diapers (ripped up sheets) and they race to diaper the guys (over their pants, of course). Or, let the guys race to see who can change a diaper on a doll the fastest.

7. *Baby Food Race.* The girls feed a jar of baby food to the guys. First to finish wins.

8. *Crying Contest.* See who can cry the loudest, most convincing, etc.

CRAZY DAZE

Decorate a bus (school bus, church bus, etc.) with poster paint, flowers, slogans, etc., or have kids decorate their cars in the same way.

The wilder the better. Then, on a Saturday or a Holiday, travel through a day of unusual small activities, none of which would be enough for an activity by itself. Examples might be to go the County Museum, a giant slide, games in the park, on a boat ride, various free tourist attractions, etc. The more short activities, the better. Have the kids decorate the bus or the cars the night before, or begin early in the morning.

FIGHT NIGHT

Have kids come in their grubbies, meet in a vacant lot or a big back yard that can be messed up real good. Rope off a square arena (about 20' by 20') and explain that all fighting will be done inside that square. Choose two boys teams and two girls teams of from 5 to 10 on a team. Boys fight each other first, then the girls. Spectators judge to determine the winners.

The events are done in rounds. The teams get in their corners (like a boxing match) and the ammo is placed in the center of the arena. When the horn or whistle sounds, they come out of the corners, grab the ammo, and start fighting until the horn blows again, which ends that round.

> Round One—Water Balloons
> Round Two—Tomatoes
> Round Three—Eggs
> Round Four—Flour
> Round Five—Mud

Make sure no kids bring any of their own ammo. You provide it all. At the end of each round, the kids go to their corners, and you bring out the eggs, or tomatoes, or whatever and place them in the middle of the arena. Check with your local grocers and there is a good chance that you can get old or spoiled merchandise for this. Mix the mud up ahead of time. Dump it in the arena with buckets or a wheelbarrow. The flour would be in little lunch bags, so that everyone on the team gets one. Rounds should be one minute in length.

Kids may wear anything they want for protection, such as football helmets, raincoats, etc. Usually they just get in the way. The winner is the cleanest team when it's all over.

Announce that no throwing of the ammo is allowed. The fighters must pick up the eggs, for example, and break them on the other person, not throw them at each other.

Be sure you have plenty of supervision, especially if you have a large number of kids on hand, or a lot of new kids. Take Super 8 movies of the action, and show them later to the kids. They won't believe they are seeing themselves. After the fights, hose everyone down with a garden hose to clean them off.

HOGWASH

A "Hogwash" is an outdoor event designed around pigs. You will need to acquire a couple of pigs from a nearby farm or school. You will also need to cage them so that they won't run off. Then choose up teams and play some of these games:

1. *Name the Pig contest.* If you have one pig for each team, let each team name their pig. Judge the best name, and give a booby prize to the worst names.

2. *Pickeled Pigs Feet Eating Contest.* Get them at a grocery store and have one person from each team race to see who can eat the most the fastest.

3. *Pig Decorating Contest.* Provide shaving cream, hats, ribbons, clothes, and whatever you have on hand, and each team decorates their pig. Set a time limit.

4. *Pig Washing Contest* (A "Hogwash"). Give each team soap, talcum powder, deodorant, etc. and each team tries to make their pig as "lovely" as possible.

5. *Tail Tie.* With all the pigs in the pen, each team has one of their players locate their pig, chase it down, and tie a ribbon on its tail.

6. *Pig Pen Contest.* This is the "Pigpen" from the famous "Peanuts" comic strip. The idea is for each team to select one of its members to decorate as ugly and dirty as possible. Use mud, dirt, old rags, charcoal, or whatever.

7. *Hog Calling Contest.* With the pigs a certain distance away, teams try to call their pig ("Soooo-eeeeeee!") in the fastest time. Pigs should be placed in the middle of the pigpen, with the kids surrounding them. This should be done one team at a time, one pig at a time.

8. *Mud Fight.* Dig a mud hole and have one minute mud fights. The cleanest team is the winner.

9. *Pig Feed.* Serve refreshments (Ice Cream, etc.) in a trough ("V" shaped, made out of wood, lined with tin foil) and kids eat without using their hands.

MAN-HUNT

This is really a "people scavenger hunt," in that the game is played just like a scavenger hunt, only the object of the hunt is people. The group meets at a central location and is divided up into teams. Each team is then given a list of kids (not names) to "bring back alive" to the meeting to be held later in the evening. The teams then go out into the neighborhood (in cars or on foot) and try to locate kids to fit the descriptions on the list, and also try to talk each person into coming back to the meeting with them. No one can be forced into coming. Each person is worth 100 points. Here is a sample list:

    A varsity football player
    An A.S.B. officer
    Someone who speaks Spanish
    A tuba player (with tuba)
    Someone who weighs over 200 pounds
    A cheerleader
    A girl with her hair in rollers
    A couple who are "going steady"
    A guy in his pajamas
    A teacher
    Someone who drives a Corvette
    Someone who has more than ten letters in his last name
    A girl with red hair
    An "A" student
    Someone who owns a guinea pig
    Someone over six feet tall
    Someone who plays a banjo

You can add more to this list, of course, or delete those that you don't like. Give kids plenty of things to choose from. The winning team is the one with the most people brought in.

The big question is: What do you do with all the people who are brought back to the meeting? One answer should be obvious. Thank them for participating, and perhaps have some refreshments available. Another answer should be equally obvious: Don't use this as your opportunity to try and convert all these kids (assuming that they are not regular members of your group). Remember that they have come ONLY as part of a fun activity, and they are *not* interested in being preached at. This event can be a good public relations activity in the sense that the new kids brought in on the hunt will get exposure to the youth group, but that is about all that you should use it for. Don't try to trap these newcomers, or to make them feel uncomfortable. Just have a good time with them.

MISSION IMPOSSIBLE

Divide the entire group into cars or buses (depending on the size of your crowd). Each group has a leader, who goes with them to make sure they don't cheat on the rules of the game which are: (1) Each team gets a list of "Impossible Missions" which they must accomplish within the given time limit. (2) They must take each mission in the order which they appear on the list. (Each list has the same missions, but arranged differently, so that everyone doesn't go on the same exact route.) (3) They cannot tell anyone they come in contact with **why** they are going about their mission until that mission has been accomplished. (In other words, they can't go up to someone and say, "Will you help us, we are playing a game, and we need. . . .") The team which completes its list of missions and returns to the starting area first, wins.

Some sample Impossible Missions:
1. Convince another teenager (off the street, or a stranger) to come

with you to help accomplish the other missions.
2. Entire group must do an Indian rain dance around the fountain at the courthouse square.
3. Get a signed statement from a doctor saying that you do not have the bubonic plague.
3. Everybody hop around the block surrounding the city park on one foot.
5. Find an on-duty policeman and report a U.F.O.
6. Find a tennis court where people are playing and each of you take a turn at hitting the ball over the net.
7. Go to a college girls dormitory and serenade the girls with "We wish you a Merry Christmas".
8. Get everyone in the group on radio or T.V., and bring back proof.
9. Talk a taxi driver into driving entire group around block for only one dollar.

(Contributed by Jerry Summers, Corpus Christi, Texas)

OLD-TIMEY NIGHT

Each kid comes to the meeting dressed in an old-fashioned outfit of some kind. (preferably 1890-ish). Award prizes for best-dressed, most authentic, etc. Prizes should be old, also, such as an 1890 Sears Catalogue, an "A-oo-gah" horn from a Model-T car, etc. Show old-time movies (W. C. Fields, Charlie Chaplin), and then perhaps after the meeting go to an ice-cream parlor, or something similar.

PEANUTS PICNIC

This special event is based on the immortal "Peanuts" comic strip characters, created by Charles Schulz, and is a great fun activity for junior highs. Advertise it as a "Peanuts Picnic," using posters, passouts, etc. incorporating the Peanuts characters as much as possible.

Refreshments can include peanuts, peanut butter sandwiches, etc. Play the games below, plus any others that you can think of that might fit the various characters, and award appropriate prizes to the winning teams. (Many stores carry a wide variety of "Peanuts" toys and gifts.)

1. *Charlie Brown's Game*: This is a game of modified softball. Play the game on a normal softball diamond, only use a "mushball", and run the bases in reverse order. The infield cannot throw the ball, but they can pick it up and run with it to tag the runner or the bases. Three innings are played, with two outs per inning. The points scored are given to the other team, and the team with the most points loses. All other rules are the same as regular softball.

2. *"Linus' Game"*: This one can also be called "Steal the Security Blanket." A blanket is placed in the center of a large square, and each team lines up on one side of the square (there should be four teams). Each team should number off 1-2-3-4-etc., so that each player has a number. To begin the game, one (or more) numbers are called out by the leader, and all the players on each team with the corresponding number(s) run to the center and try to pull the blanket across their team's side of the square. As soon as any part of the blanket crosses their side, a point is scored and the blanket is returned to the center of the square and the players return to their sides. A new number or numbers is called and the game is over as soon as everyone is sick and tired of playing it. For best results, use a "blanket" made of very tough material, like canvas.

3. *"Snoopy's Game"*: This is a "doghouse pack," which requires the acquisition of or the building of a "doghouse." Each team simply tries to see how many kids they can pack inside and on top of the doghouse within a given time limit. The team that gets the most kids in and on it is the winner.

4. *"Red Baron vs. Snoopy Game"*: This game should be played on a large open field, or in an open wooded area. Draw a line of demarcation which separates the Red Baron's territory from Snoopy's territory. The group is divided in half, with all the "Red Barons" in their territory and all the "Snoopys" in their territory. Each player on the Snoopy team has a "tail," which can be a flag (like those used in flag football) or a piece of tape on their clothing. Before the game begins, the Snoopys gather at the end of their territory, as far away from the line of demarcation as possible, and the Red Barons line up on the line. On a signal, the Snoopy players try to get into Red Baron territory with their tails still on, and the Red Baron players try to capture tails before they cross the line. The Snoopy team gets a point for every tail they get into Red Baron territory, and the Red Baron team gets a point for each tail they capture.

5. *"Schroeder's Game"*: Schroeder is the little boy who loves to play his little toy piano, and this game is a musical one. Each team must compose and perform a short team "song." A panel of judges selects the winner.

6. *"Pig Pen's Game":* Each team decorates one member of their team to look like the "Pig Pen" character. Mud, grease, dirt, charcoal, marking pens, torn clothes, etc., may be used to make the kid look as dirty as possible. A panel of judges can select the winner.

7. *"Lucy's Psychiatric Treatment Skit":* Send several kids out of the room and bring them in one at a time for the "Psychological Story" (see page 39) or the "Psychiatrist Skit" (found on page 153).

POSTER CONTEST

Choose up teams, and each team gets a stack of magazines, magic markers, poster paints, poster board, rubber cement, etc., and from these materials, each team is to make posters describing some special event. Winning posters are chosen for originality, humor, etc., and appropriate prizes are awarded. This is a good way to get kids involved in the advertising of your program. (Contributed by Jerry Summers, Corpus Christi, Texas)

RACE RIOT

Have an evening of different types of races. For example: a foot race, a wheelbarrow race, a VW race, a sack race, etc. Advertise it as a "Race Riot," be creative, and this can be a winner.

TREASURE HUNTS

The "Treasure Hunt" has been an old stand-by for many years, but it has rarely been done well. The following is a guide to enable you to creatively inject new life into this old idea, and make it an exciting experience every time you use it (Yes, you *can* use it more than once!).

The first thing to remember is that by giving the event a new name, you make it a new event. For example, rather than calling it a Treasure Hunt, make the treasure a live goose hidden somewhere, and call it a "Wild Goose Chase." Or the object of the hunt might be a snowman that you built somewhere in town, and you can then have a "Search for the Abominable Snowman." One group obtained a live Hippopotamus and had a "Hippo Hunt." All the kids wore safari hats and followed the clues to the hippo which was tied up in the middle of the city's largest shopping center. This is where your own creativity becomes important. The possibilities are endless. Just don't rely on the same old thing over and over again.

In case you are not familiar with the basics of a treasure hunt, the idea is for participants to locate the "treasure," and be the first to do so. This is done by solving a number of "clues" that are placed in different locations, with each clue leading to another clue and then finally to the "treasure" itself.

The Hunt Begins:
Have everyone meet at a certain time and place and assign them all to cars or busses (depending on the size of the crowd). Have each vehicle appoint a leader or captain and then have a brief meeting with each of the captains to explain the rules and begin the hunt. The rules should include the following:

1. Time Limit. At a certain time the hunt is over regardless of whether or not the treasure has been found. Usually two hours is plenty of time for most hunts.

2. Explanation of the "Clue Packet."

3. The first clue is given to the captains at this time. The clue is sealed in an envelope, and when you give the signal (whistle or racing flag, etc.) the clues are opened and the hunt is off and running. Each captain opens the clues, takes it to his team and as soon as they figure out the clue, they go where the clue takes them.

The Clues:
Each vehicle should be numbered, and in your planning of the hunt, you should plan for each vehicle to take a different route to the treasure. That prevents the groups from simply following each other. Each vehicle should go to all of the same places, just in a different

order.

Each clue will take the vehicle to one of six locations (more or less if you want). The last location is where the treasure is. The winner must decipher all the clues as well as locate the treasure. If you somehow are able to cheat and locate the treasure without working out all the clues, you are penalized. Each clue leads to the next clue, and you must take them in order.

At each location, there is someone with the clues (a sponsor or youth leader not participating in the hunt itself). The clues are numbered so that each group gets the right clue to keep them on the right course. Sometimes it adds to the fun to have the "Clue Giver" hidden at the clue location, and the kids have to find him in some way. For example, if the location is a restaurant, the "Clue Giver" might be sitting at a table eating. The kids must find him by saying the "secret word" to everyone in the place, until they get the right response (and the clue) from the right person. Of course, if you do this, you need to use someone that the kid's won't recognize. Also, be sure and get permission to do this from the owners of the restaurant, store, etc.

Make the clues hard. Unless the kids are very young, they can usually figure out a lot more than we think. They can take many forms, such as these samples actually used in a treasure hunt in San Diego, California:

1. An envelope containing an egg yoke and a piece of ham. (Yoke plus ham equals "yokahama," or a landmark in San Diego called the "Yokahama Bell.")

2. A piece of paper with the letters "IIDEORPS," which, when unscrambled, spell out a park in San Diego called "Presidio" park.

3. A list of numbers: 23456
   26576
   67934
   94376

When the numbers are added up, they give a phone number, and they are to go to a phone booth and use the dime in the "clue packet" to call the number and find the next location.

4. A set of instructions for the team captains:

   a. Divide the entire group up into four small groups and give each small group one of these sounds:

      LLL
      DUH
      SEE
      WHR

   b. Have the groups combine sounds until they make sense. (Sea World)

Clue Packets:

Each group is given a manila envelope full of things that may or may not be important to them. They get the packet at the beginning of the hunt and the captains are instructed to familiarize themselves with its contents immediately. Here are some suggestions for things to go in the clue packet:

1. *The Hunt Map.* (An ordinary road map). The map is marked with numbers and arrows pointing to certain locations. ONLY the locations marked are possible clue locations. They may not be a clue location, but only the marked ones are possibilities.

2. *Rules* (Basic instructions).

3. *General clue sheet.* This sheet contains clue phrases that may or may not be important to the clues. If a group is having a difficult time with a certain clue they should check the general clue sheet to see if it will help. Example phrases might be:

   a. The first two letters are all you need.
   b. Shamu lives there.
   c. Blue is a pretty color.

4. *General clue items.* General clue items are odds and ends that may or may not be of help in solving some or all of the clues. Items could be punched IBM cards, a dime, bandaid, etc.

5. *Emergency Clues.* If a group is unable to figure out their clue, then they can open an amergency clue, which is very easy, and continue the hunt. However, each vehicle is penalized 15 minutes for each emergency clue used. The emergency clues are numbered and sealed in envelopes just like the regular clues and they must be turned in at the treasure location. If any are opened, then they must wait out their penalty time before they can claim the treasure. If another group arrived during that pen-

We're going to have a HIPPO HUNT

alty time with no emergency clues opened, they would win.

Some Reminders:

If the treasure is not found, the winner is determined by who got the farthest using the least amount of emergency clues. This really should not happen, though. Plan enough time that everyone will get to the treasure.

If the treasure itself is not something that the kids can keep, then have some appropriate prizes to give to the winning group. Have a presentation of the hunt "trophy" to the team captain, and make a big deal out of this.

Don't use the same kind of clue each time. Make them all different, and a new challenge with each clue. This adds tremendously to a good hunt.

Clue locations should be as unusual as possible, such as the top of a church tower, a boat in the middle of a lake, up in a tree, buried in a cemetery, at a tourist attraction, etc.

Make sure speed and traffic laws are obeyed. The drivers should be carefully screened to avoid problems in this area. Make sure drivers have necessary permissions from parents (if they are kids), insurance, and a drivers license. One group put a sponsor in each vehicle who held a spoon with an egg (raw) in it out the window. If the vehicle went too fast, bounced, swerved, etc., the egg would drop and break. Each vehicle started with a dozen eggs, and they were penalized for each egg broken during the hunt.

COME TO A... WILD GOOSE CHASE!

It is usually a good idea to have the last place (the location of the treasure) somewhere suitable for a meeting. After all the kids are back from the hunt, they can share experiences, you can award prizes, perhaps have some singing, crowd breakers, or a speaker, and some refreshments.

WEDNESDAY NIGHT AT THE MOVIES

The day in the title can be changed to match any day of the week you decide to hold this event. All the kids in your group are urged to bring old home movies (sports, baby, family, cartoons, etc.). Line up projectors (3 or more) and sheets or screens. The idea is to have several films going at once on different walls or side by side on a long wall, allowing kids to mingle around and view the film they like. This creates an "art-film" atmosphere. Set up a popcorn stand, coke machine, etc. The results are fantastic.

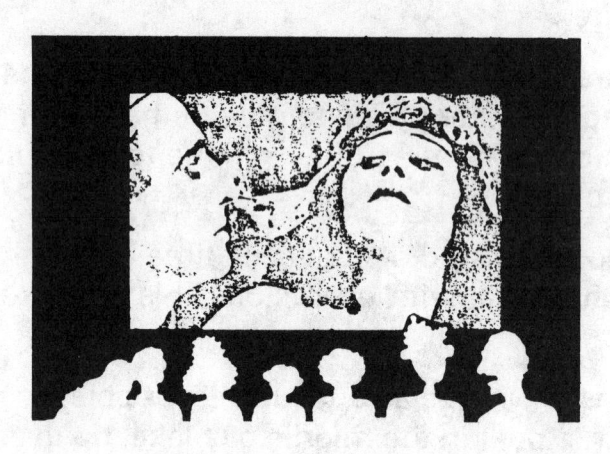

Chapter Six

Skits

AN EVENING WITH GRANDMA

This is a spoof on melodramas that is a lot of fun and requires no acting ability at all. In fact, no lines are spoken. The narrator simply reads the script, and the characters (as listed below) do as they are instructed in the footnotes following the script. The most difficult part is getting together all the props you need, but more are very easy to obtain. Encourage the characters to really ham it up and have fun. It is almost guaranteed to be a winner, especially at camps.

The Characters: (Not including the narrator)
1. Manuel—should be dressed in black
2. Maggie—should be dressed in old fashioned dress
3. Patrick—should be in white
4. Zingerella—dressed like a housekeeper
5. and 6. Two people to be the "curtains" (They hold signs to that effect).
7. and 8. Two people to be the "hours" (They also have signs)
9. The sun (boy or girl)
10. Night (boy or girl)

Props Needed:
1. Pitcher of Water
2. A podium
3. Chalk
4. Trading or Postage Stamps
5. Broom
6. Pail (Bucket)
7. Banana
8. Police whistle
9. Iron
10. Rope
11. Salt shakers (2)
12. Large wooden match
13. Notes
14. Signs (below):
   a. Curtains (2)
   b. Stairs
   c. Time
   d. No (30 or more)
   e. Hours (2)
   f. Sun
   g. Night

The Script: To be read by the narrator as the characters act according to instructions given in the footnotes.

The curtains part.[1]
The sun rises.[2]
Our play begins.
Manuel de Populo, son of a wealthy merchant, is in his study, care-

fully pouring over his notes.[3] He stamps his feet[4] impatiently, and calls for his maid, Zingerella.

Zingerella tears down the stairs[5] and trips into the room.[6] "Go fetch Maggie O'Toole," demands Manuel, Zingerella flies[7] to do her master's bidding.

Time passes[8]

Manuel crosses the floor—once—twice—thrice[9] At last Maggie comes sweeping into the room.[10]

"For the last time, will you marry me?" insists Manuel. Maggie turns a little pale.[11]

"NO," she shouts, "A thousand times NO."[12]

Then I will have to cast you into the dungeon, says Manuel, in a rage.

She throws herself at his feet.[13] "Oh Sir," she pleads, "I appeal to you."[14]

Haughtily he says, "Your appeal is fruitless.[15]" At that, Manuel stomps out of the room.[16]

Maggie flies about in a dither.[17] Oh, if only Patrick would come, he would save her!

The hours pass slowly.[18] Finally Maggie takes her stand,[19] and scans[20] the horizon. Suddenly she hears a whistle.[21] Could it be . . .???

"Maggie, it is I, my love, your Patrick!!!"

He enters the room and tenderly presses her hand.[22] She throws him a line.[23] Just at that moment, Manuel re-enters and challenges Patrick to a duel. In a fury, they assault each other.[24] Finally Manuel gives up the match,[25] and departs. "At last, you are mine!" says Patrick. He leads his love away into the night.[26] The sun sets.[27] Night Falls.[28] The curtains come together[29] and our play is ended.

Footnotes:

1. Two people with signs that say "curtains" walk away from each other beginning at center of the stage.
2. Person with "sun" sign, stands up.
3. He pours water from a pitcher all over some notes.
4. Licks stamps, sticks on shoes.
5. Rips down a sign that says "stairs" and tears it up.
6. Falls down. (trips)
7. Waves arms in flying motion.
8. Guy holding "time" sign walks across stage.
9. Takes chalk and makes three big "X's" on the floor.
10. Sweeps with a broom.
11. Turns a pail upside down.
12. Throws paper with "no" on them.
13. Falls at his feet and lies there.
14. Hands him a banana peel.
15. Hands the banana peel back.
16. Stomps his feet.

17. Waves arms in flying manner.
18. Two people with "hours" signs walk across the stage.
19. Stands behind podium.
20. Hand above eyes in searching motion.
21. Patrick blows police whistle.
22. Takes iron and irons her hand.
23. Throws a rope at him.
24. Take salt shakers and sprinkle each other.
25. Hands Patrick a wooden match.
26. Bump into the guy with the night sign.
27. Sun sits down.
28. "Night" falls down.
29. "Curtains" walk toward each other.

An Evening with Grandma

CROP DUSTER

This is an interview skit which requires two people. Lines should be memorized and rehearsed for timing. Costumes should be simple. The interviewer only needs a trenchcoat and a microphone. "Dusty" should look as ridiculous as possible. An old World War I pilot's cap and goggles, combat boots, and props that the skit calls for are all you need. Use your own creativity here.

Interviewer:
Today it is our privilege to have with us one of the men who made America great. Risking life and limb daily, he pursues his dangerous task with the very calm and cool nerve borne only of a man who is truly one of the great adventurers of modern times. He is the skill that has contributed so much to the wealth and beauty of our country and the abundance of our harvest. A real warm hand for one of California's foremost crop dusters . . . Dusty Crashalot!
(Enter Dusty, throwing flour from a paper bag)

Int: Well, it's really great to have you with us today, Dusty, Just how long have you been a cropduster?

Dusty: Well, let's see now . . . mmm . . . ah . . . two weeks. Yeah, that's right. Two weeks!

Int: Two weeks? Well, that's not a very long time.

Dusty: Well, a cropduster's life expectancy isn't very long either. We can only get one kind of insurance you know.

Int: Oh. You can get insurance? I thought your job was so dangerous that you couldn't get insurance.

Dusty: Oh yes. I'm fully covered for childbirth.

Int: I see. Dusty, were you ever a commercial pilot before you became a cropduster?

Dusty: Oh yes. I was a pilot on a cattle ranch.

Int: A cattle ranch? What does a pilot on a cattle ranch do?

Dusty: Oh, I just pilot here, pilot there, just piling it wherever I can pilot (makes like a shovel)

Int: Well, I meant, didn't you ever fly an airplane?

Dusty: (Pulls paper airplane from pocket) Oh, yes, why I flew one all the way from the back of the room to the blackboard once.

Int: No, I mean while you dust crops. Don't you fly an airplane while you dust crops?

Dusty: Oh, no, that would be too dangerous. You have to have your hands free to dip in the sack!

Int: I see . . . but . . .

Dusty: Well, I guess you could fly the plane with your feet, but you sure can't dip in the sack with your feet!

Int: What kind of equipment do you use in your work, Dusty?

Dusty: Well, usually a whisk broom, or a feather-duster. I just walk up and down the rows dusting off the plants. They have to breathe, you know!

Int: You actually dust the crops with a feather-duster?

Dusty: Well, once I used one of my wife's wigs. But she blew her top over that!

Int: What is the main crop that you dust, Dusty?

Dusty: Well, let's see . . . that would be the Potunge!

Int: What is a potunge?

Dusty: Well, it's a cross between a potato and a sponge.

Int: Sounds interesting. Does it taste good?

Dusty: No, it tastes terrible, but, man, it sure soaks up the gravy!

Int: Dusty, do you ever work in cotton?

Dusty: No, most of my underclothes are Japanese silk!

Int: Dusty, tell us about your most exciting experience as a crop duster.

Dusty: Well, that would be when I saw so high in my plane, that the field below looked like a Postage Stamp. I sent my plane into a power dive and crashed to earth.

Int: Did you hit the field?

Dusty: What field? It **was** a postage stamp!

Int: Have you ever had any other experiences like that, Dusty?

Dusty: Well, that would be the time when my plane lost its power at 10,000 feet.

Int: Really? That's bad!

Dusty: Not too bad. I had my chute on.

Int: That's good.

Dusty: Not too good. It wouldn't open.

Int: Oooooh . . . that's bad!

Dusty: Not too bad. I was headed straight for a haystack.

Int: Well, that's good.

Dusty: No, that was bad! There was a pitchfork in the haystack.

Int: Oh, that is bad.

Dusty: Not too bad . . . I missed the pitchfork.

Int: That's good.

Dusty: No, that's bad. I missed the haystack too!!

FRONTIER MORTICIAN

The following skit is one of the classics. It is a skit that should be rehearsed, staged, memorized, and properly presented rather than simply read. Characters required:
1. The Announcer (Ann.)
2. Sam Alamode
3. Piney "Pie" Alamode
4. Trigger Mortis (Trig.)
5. Joe Silver
6. Arnie

Ann: The makers of Fatrical present (MUSIC)—Frontier Mortician . . . Are you skinny and run down? Are you so thin you have to wear skis in the bathtub to keep from going down the drain? When you turn sideways and stick out your tongue, do you look like a zipper? When you drink strawberry pop, do you look like a thermometer? Then you need Fatrical—the drink that adds weight to you. Fatrical is not a capsule, it is not a solid, it is not a liquid—it's a gas that you inhale. Fatrical comes in one delicious gas flavor—mustard. It costs only $4.95 a case, and the equipment for inhaling it costs only $5,678. This includes a 10,000 cubic foot tank, 300 feet of hose, three pumps, two filter tips, and a partridge in a pear tree. Now for our story—Trigger Mortis, Frontier Mortician. The scene opens in the residence of Sam Alamode, wealthy rancher and owner of the Bar B Q ranch in Sparerib, Texas. Sam is dying and is talking to his lovely daughter Piney Alamode, whom he lovingly calls Pie . . .

Sam: Pie, honey, I'm dying again. Go call Trigger Mortis, the frontier mortician. Have hearse will travel.

Pie: What's wrong with you, daddy? What's your ailment?

Sam: I swallowed the thermomenter and I'm dying by degrees.

Pie: I'll go call Trigger Mortis right now . . .

Ann: Unknown to Sam Alamode, his head foreman, Joe Silver, is hiding outside listening to the conversation. He's a fullblooded Indian, and Sam always called him his faithful Indian companion Silver. Sam doesn't hear Joe speak . . .

Joe: Let old Sam die. I wish he would. Then I can get the ranch and be set for life. He's always got some fool disease. Last week he swallowed a dynamite cap and his hair came out in bangs. Before that he swallowed a hydrogen bomb and had atomic ache. He's suffering from flower disease—he's a blooming idiot. Hey—here comes Pie Alamode's stupid boyfriend, Arnie. Poor kid . . . he's an orphan . . . litle orphan Arnie . . . I'll just sneak away . . .

Arnie: I haven't seen my girlfriend Pie Alamode for two weeks. Boy, she has lovely eyes—one is brown and other two are blue. Last time she rolled her eyes at me, and I picked them up and rolled them back. I remember the first time she kissed me . . . it made chills go up and down my spine . . . then I found out her popcicle was leaking. I'll knock at the door. (KNOCKS)

Pie: Who is it?

Arnie: It's me, honey—and I call you honey cause you have hives.

Pie: Oh, my cookie . . . and I call you cookie because you're so crummy.

Ann: We interrupt this love scene to bring you a message from Peter Pan makeup. Use Peter Pan before your pan peters out. This is the makeup used by the stars—Lassie, Gentle Ben, and Phyllis Diller. Listen to this letter from Mrs. Mergatroid Fluglehorn from Liverlip, Mississippi: "My face was so wrinkled I had to screw my hat on. Then I used Peter Pan makeup and I don't look like an old woman anymore—I look like an old man. I had my wrinkles tightened up, and now every time I raise my eyebrows, I pull up my socks. I give all the credit to Peter Pan . . ." You can be beautiful, too . . . now back to Frontier Mortician . . . Trigger Mortis, the fronter mortician, is answering his telephone . . .

Trig: Oh, it's you, Miss Pie Alamode. You want me to come to see your father? Well, my hearse has been giving me trouble—I think I blew a casket. I've got to quit using embalming fluid in the gas tank, becuase the motor keeps dying. Yes . . . yes . . . well, I have to finish my breakfast. I'm eating Shrouded Wheat and Ghost Toasties . . . Well, I'll hurry right out. Goodbye—I must be shovelling off . . .

Ann: Pie Alamode hangs up and goes to meet her lover, little orphan Arnie, in their favorite meeting place . . . the family graveyard.

Pie: It's so romantic here in the graveyard. There's the grave of my Uncle Earnest. Look . . . there are some maggots making love in dead earnest.

Arnie: Darling, may I have your hand in marriage?

Pie: My hand—oh, yes. In fact, you can have my arm, too.

Arnie: Here, I'll put this ring on your finger.

Pie: Awwww, your face is turning red.

Arnie: Yeah, and your finger's turning green . . . after all, we've been going together for twelve years now.

Pie: So what do you want—a pension . . . let's go tell my father.

Ann: This program is brought to you by the Double Insanity Insurance Company. Mothers, do you have children? Then protect them with a double deal policy. We pay $100,000 if your son is killed by a herd of white elephants going east on Thursday. If you lose an arm, we help you look for it. If you get hit in the head, we pay you in one lump sum. We have a double indemnity clause, too—if you die in an accident, we bury you twice. Now, a report from the National Safety Council. It is predicted that 356 people will die in accidents this week-end. So far only 135 have been reported. Some of you aren't trying . . . Now, back to our story. Joe Silver is plotting to kidnap Pie Alamode and hold her for ransom. He thinks Sam Alamode is dying, but he really isn't. Trigger Mortis, frontier mortician, is on his way to the ranch . . .

Trig: Well, here I am. When you are at death's door, I will pull you through.

Sam: Good to see you, Trigger. Can you give me a good funeral?

Trig: I'll give you a good funeral or your mummy back. Could I interest you in our new layaway plan?

Sam: I'm a sick man, a sick man. The doctor told me to drink some medicine after a hot bath, and I can hardly finish drinking the bath.

Trig: You need some of my Whistler's Mother medicine—one dose and you're off your rocker.

Sam: Trigger, I can trust you, can't I?

Trig: Of corpse, of corpse . . . have I ever let you down?

Sam: I don't trust my faithful Indian companion, Silver. He has a sneaky look.

Trig: I happen to know, Sam, that Joe Silver wants to kidnap your daughter and keep her from marrying little orphan Arnie.

Sam: Trigger, we gotta do something. Think of a plan.

Ann: Will Trigger Mortis think of a plan? While he thinks, a word from Honest John Pendergast, the used car dealer. Honest John has bargains in used cars that you can't afford to miss. Here's an 1887 Essex—this is a revolutionary car—Washington drove it at Vally Forge. The tires are so beat that you not only knock the pedestrians down, you whip them to death. This car has low lines—in fact, it's so low it doesn't have doors—it has manhole covers . . . This program is also brought to you by Glum, the toothpaste that gives your bad breath the Good Housekeeping seal of approval. Are your teeth like the Ten Commandments—all broken? Do you have a Pullman car mouth—one upper and one lower? Then use Glum . . . Glum contains eucalyptus oil, flown in from Australia. This eucalyptus oil is the secret of Glum. Millions of users say, "Man, you clipt us." Be true to your teeth and they will never be false to you. Now, back to Frontier Mortician. Sam, Pie, Arnie, and Trigger Mortis are trying to figure out how to get rid of Joe Silver.

Sam: I have a splitting headache.

Trig: Have your eyes ever been checked?

Sam: No, they've always been blue . . . Trigger, why don't we put Joe in one of your coffins and ship him out of the state?

Trig: A tisket, a tasket, I'll put him in a casket. I was in love once, so I

Pie: know what Arnie and Pie are going through.

Pie: You were in love?

Trig: Yes . . . I was stuck on a girl who worked in the glue factory. She had a schoolgirl complexion . . . with diplomas under her eyes. Her lips were like petals . . . bicycle pedals. Those lips . . . those teeth . . . that hair . . . that eye . . .

Arnie: Hey—here comes Joe Silver. Get your coffin ready, Trigger.

Pie: Daddy, lie on the bed and act like you're dead.

Ann: Sam lies on the bed and holds his breath. Trigger takes off his shoes and everybody holds their breath . . . At this breathless moment, we bring you the daily police calls. Calling car 15, calling car 15—happy birthday, car 15, you are now car 16. Car 56, car 56, rush to the Bungling Brother's Circus. The fat woman has hay fever and is crying so much three midgets are about to drown. Car 23, car 23—return the 10-gallon hat bought for the mayor—he has an 11-gallon head. Car 19, go to the corner of 6th and Main—the Chinese cook has just committed chop sueycide . . . back to the story. Joe Silver enters Sam's bedroom as the other people hide.

Joe: So I finally caught you, you scroundrel. You've cut my check so many times I have to endorse it with Mercurochrome. I want to marry your daughter, Sam, and nobody's gonna stop me. Sure I'm tough . . . I've been sent up the river so many times I get fan mail from the salmon. The last time they caught me I got ten years in jail and two in the electric chair. Even when I was a baby people were pinning things on me. Now, I'm gonna get you.

Sam: Get him Arnie.

Trig: Quick, I have the casket opened. Push him, Arnie.

Joe: Help—help—you're pushing me . . . (MUFFLED SOUNDS)

Trig: That takes care of him. Now I have to run for a body. A fellow in town swallowed a quart of shellac and died . . . he had a lovely finish.

Arnie: How can we thank you? You'll come to the wedding, won't you?

Trig: Yes, I plan to give you a tombstone for a present, but don't take it for granite.

Sam: Thanks, Trig. By the way, stop over and we'll play golf someday.

Trig: Don't ever play golf with an undertaker—he's always on top at the last hole.

Arnie: Now we're alone, Pie, my love. Someday you'll have my name.

Pie: I never did find out—what is your last name, Arnie?

Arnie: My name is Arnie R. Square.

Pie: What a lovely name I'll have—Mrs. Pie R. Square.

Ann: And as the sun sinks slowly in the west, we leave the lovers as they plan their future. Tune in tomorrow for a new adventure, brought to you by Bleeties, the cereal for old goats. Bleeties contains 56% iron, 22% copper, 78% steel, 14% bronze, and 11% zinc. It doesn't snap, crackle, or pop—it lies there and rusts. Bleeties isn't the breakfast of champions—it's for people who just want to get into the semi-finals. In closing, be sure to visit your local dime store where they're having a monster sale. Haven't you always wanted to own your own monster? We have vampires at special prices and they're excellent for curing tired blood! These are experienced vampires who all worked as tellers in blood banks. Now . . . tune in tomorrow for the first episode of the new story, "I was a Teen-age Spinster" brought to you by the gardener's magazine, Weeder's Digest.

HERKIMER THE ALL AMERICAN

This skit requires two people: The coach (interviewer) and the football player, Herkimer (the interviewee). Costumes should be simple but appropriate. All the coach needs is a whistle, hat, etc. and Herkimer should look as ridiculous as possible wearing old football gear.

Coach: Hi everyone! It's good to be here to tell you a little about the inside of football. What players think and how plays are really born. All of the really hard work of making a good football team. At this time I would like to introduce one of our real star players to help inform you! (Yells off stage 'HERKIMER' . . . enter big player with little boys uniform and helmet on backward—also girls purse tucked in pants so audience can't see it).

Coach: Aw come on Herk, you got your helmet on backwards.

Herk: Well, you told me I was gonna be a catcher and I don't want to get hit in the nose!

Coach: I didn't say catcher. I said an end who catches passes. Look, Herk, I think I made a mistake putting you at end.

Herk: Wadda ya mean mistake, last game I had three completes in a row.

Coach: Ya I know Herk, but we call them interceptions when the other team gets it!

Herk: Gee Coach, you said don't let the ball touch the ground and that big guy said he had it so I thought 'let him have it.'

Coach: Ok Herk, but I'm gonna change you anyway cause you're just not rough enough!

Herk: Not rough enough! Last game I got in a fight right on the field.

Coach: You did? What happened—did somebody hit you?

Herk: Ya . . . this big guy (pulls out purse) . . . so I just took my purse and beat him (starts beating coach)

Coach: Ok, ok, Herk, but I'm gonna change you to a half back anyway!

Herk: Oh please Coach, not that—I need all my back. It's not very big anyway!

Coach: No, Herk, it's a position on the field. Here, let me show you a play . . . (has a play diagrammed on board . . . x's and o's). Ya see, Herk, you take the ball from the quarterback. This man blocks here, this one there, and this one here, then you run for a touchdown!

Herk: Really—ME!!

Coach: Sure—you! Do you have any questions?

Herk: Just one—what are all those x's and o's?

Coach: Forget it! Here, let me give you our schedule so you can really get jazzed up! (Herk starts pawing ground and snorting). Next week we play the Brownies!

Herk: The Brownies—WOW!

Coach: The next week the Girl Scouts (Herk comments— Really!!') After that the Bluebirds.

Herk: BLUEBIRDS! THE VARSITY!

Coach: And our last game is the Los Angeles Rams!

Herk: Nyaaa!

Coach: Does anyone on that list scare you?

Herk: Just one . . . THE BLUEBIRDS.

Coach: Ya, ya. Well, they do have pretty tough girls!

Herk: (fiendish look in his eye) Ya, they sure do!

Coach: No, not that kind of tough! Well, Herk, we're running out of time. Is there anything you would like to pass on to the young boys that would help them?

Herk: Daaa ya—just take that old football and tuck it under your arm (puts nose near underarm and indicates terrible odor). On second thought better not do that—it'll rot! Carry it out here (grips it with fingertips, arms outstretched) and just GO GO GO! (runs out)

Coach: Let's give Herk a hand! Well, as you can see Herk isn't too sharp but let me tell you about the sharpest thing around! (Announcement . . .)

THE KING AND QUEEN OPERA

This is a skit which is to be performed entirely by two guys. It **can be done** by as many as five people, however, as there are five different characters or "parts" in the skit. However, part of the fun and success of this skit is watching the two guys who are performing jump in and out of costumes as they switch off parts. In other words, the two guys are actually playing all five parts.

Props for the play are very simple. All that is needed is three chairs or "thrones" for the king, queen, and princess. An optional prop is a "gate" which can be as simple as a pole with a sign on it that says "gate."

Costumes should be very simple and easy to get on and off. When they are not in use they are just laid in place on the chairs or on the ground. When the guys finish being one person, they take off one costume and jump into another as fast as possible. Part of the humor is watching the guys get the costumes on wrong or backwards, etc. Some suggested costumes are:

- Knight: Shield, sword, helmet, chest plate, made out of cardboard and tin foil.
- Servant: Dumb-looking hat, glasses, jacket, etc.
- King: A gold crown, sceptor, and robe (bathrobe).
- Queen: Old-fashioned dress, black mop wig, glasses, etc.
- Princess: Formal gown, blonde wig, high heels, etc.

It is best to have a pianist who can accompany the guys as they sing.

(Sorry, but we don't have the musical scores to the tunes listed below. These are ordinary pop tunes that any music stores would carry if the pianist or guys don't know the songs.) The guys should really ham it up as they sing, imitating operatic singers, and singing in a high falsetto for the female parts.

As the skit opens, the servant is standing by the "gate," and the Knight enters:

KNIGHT	*(Habanera)*	Oh, I would like to see the King The King it is whom I'd like to see I've traveled far o'er hill and valley I would like to see his Majesty.
SERVANT	*(Habanera)*	Wait right here and I'll ask him Wait right here and I'll ask the King Wait right here you big dumb knight And I'll go and ask the King.
KNIGHT		Well hurry up . . .
SERVANT		Oh I will not!
KNIGHT		Get the lead out of your leotards!
SERVANT		I'll take my time . . .
KNIGHT		Oh, no you'll not, or else I'll haaave your head! *(Knight becomes the King)*
SERVANT	*(Pomp and Circumstance)*	King, Ohhhhh King, King ohhh King A man awaits, without the gate A man awaits, without the gate A man awaits, without the gate
KING	*(Pomp and Circumstance)*	. . . Well, give him the gate, give him the gate. *(King becomes Knight)*
SERVANT	*(Pomp and Circumstance)*	Man, ohhh man . . . Man, ohh man, King says to give you . . . To give you the gate, King says to give you, give you the gate!
KNIGHT	*(If I Loved You)*	If I stabbed you, blood it would flow in an oozy way *(Stabs servant; dead servant becomes King)*
KNIGHT	*(Somewhere Over the Rainbow)*	King, I'd like to have your daughter's hand, In Marriage . . . and the rest of her, and the rest of her too.
KING		If you will wait right here my man, I'll ask the Queen of our daughter's plan for you . . . *(Knight becomes Queen)* Ohh, Queenie dear, my dear, my dear . . . A man waits here, waits here, waits here, to marry our sweet daughter.
QUEEN	*(Somewhere Over the Rainbow)*	I'll just have to ask her what she thinks She may think that he's charming, or she may think he stinks. *(King becomes Princess)*
QUEEN	*(O, Sole Mio)*	A man is waiting to marry you, please tell us daughter what you want to do.

PRINCESS	(O, Sole Mio)	You may tell him, that for my sake, I'd like to see him jump in the lake. *(Princess becomes King)*
QUEEN	(You Did It)	She doesn't want to do it, to do it, to do it, She had her chance and blew it, oh, yes she did. Tell the man who's waiting, he'll have to blow 'cause our daughter, she says her answer's No! *(Queen becomes Knight)*
KING	(Irene)	I'm sorry, sorry but . . . our daughter's answer is No. Tonight you might have been married, but now you might as well blow.
KNIGHT	(Irene)	I'm very sorry too, very sorry too, because my disappointment must be taken out on you. *(Stabbed King becomes Queen)*
KNIGHT	(Some Enchanted Evening)	Some enchanted evening, I would like to marry your sweet, charming daughter, and take her home with me . . .
QUEEN	(Some Enchanted Evening)	If you'll wait right here, I'll speak to the dear and see what she thinks of the o-o-offer . . . *(Knight becomes Princess)*
QUEEN	(Some Enchanted Evening)	Here's a man my dearie, who would like to marry Here's a man my dearie, who would like to marry . . .
PRINCESS	(Some Enchanted Evening)	You may tell him, mother, that I am not interested, I want him like I want a hole in my head . . . *(Princess becomes Knight)*
QUEEN	(Some Enchanted Evening)	Our daughter says No, you might as well blow You'll nevermore see her again and again.
KNIGHT	(Some Enchanted Evening)	You should not have said that, no, no, no, no, no, no . . . But since you have said it you're going to have to go *(Dead Queen becomes Princess)*
KNIGHT	(Three Blind Mice)	Marry me, marry me; marry me, marry me . . . I want to have you marry, I want to have you marry me . . . Please don't say NO . . . Please don't say No.
PRINCESS	(Three Blind Mice)	No, no, no, no, no, no, no, no, no, no, no, no, I do not want to marry you, I do not want to marry you. The answer's no, the answer's No. *(Repeat round)*
KNIGHT & PRINCESS		Hallelujah Chorus
KNIGHT	(I've Grown Accustomed to Your Face)	I'm unaccustomed to a No Well the answer's quite a blow This so very unexpected and it makes me very sad Since it's eye for eyeball, I will have to act real bad Since you won't be my wife,

> I'll stab you with my knife,
> I'll stab you with my knife—
> It's quite accustomed to a blow.
> *(Stabs Princess)*

KNIGHT   *(Do, Re, Mi)*
> I have killed a lot of folks
> there's the servant lying there
> And the King is next to him . . .
> And the Queen, the Queen so fair . . .
> There's the lovely Princess, too;
> Killing her has made me blue—
> Might as well kill myself too,
> Scooby, scooby, dooby doo!

LEAVING HOME

A man sits in a chair reading a newspaper. A woman enters with a coat on and carrying a suitcase. She is apparently very upset. The man in the chair could care less.

Woman: I've had it! I'm through! I'm leaving this crummy rotten house and all these crummy kids and going home to mother! I'm sick and tired of ironing, mopping and cleaning up after you day in and day out! I tell you, I've had it! No more! I'm leaving and don't ask me to come back because I am leaving for good! (sobbing) Good bye! (stomps out of the room)

Man: (somewhat bewildered, turns to an offstage room and yells) Alice, dear! The maid just quit.

LITTLE RED RIDING HOOD

The following skit requires only two characters. One is a guy dressed up like "Little Red Riding Hood" (A red raincoat with a hood or a red scarf should be worn.) The other is the wolf (dressed in black). Little Red has a basket covered with a towel. Inside the basket is a blank (starter's) gun. Little Red skips into the room with her basket . . .

Red: (to audience) I'm Little Red Riding Hood and I'm going to gramma's house with this basket of goodies! (skips around the stage area)

The wolf enters.

Wolf: (jumps in front of Red) Boo!

Red: EEK! EEK! Boy are you ugly!

Wolf: I'm the big bad wolf and I'm going to eat you all up!

Red: But I'm just poor Little Red Riding Hood and I'm going to gramma's house with this basket of goodies. You wouldn't want to disappoint poor old gramma now, would you?

Wolf: You got a point there. I'll let you go this time. Maybe I'll run into the three pigs somewhere along the way.

> Red Riding Hood skips off around the room and the wolf turns to the audience and says:

Wolf: Ha Ha Ha, What Little Red Riding Hood doesn't know is that I'm gonna beat her to gramma's house. I'll take a shortcut through the strawberry patch . . . sort of a "strawberry shortcut . . ."

> The wolf gets under a blanket on the floor and Red Riding Hood arrives.

Red: Knock! Knock!

Wolf: Who's there? (in a high voice)

Red: Yah!

Wolf: Yah-who! Aw, just come on in already.

Red: Hi, gramma. Gee, what big ears you have, gramma.

Wolf: What? Oh, yeah . . . all the better to hear you with, my dear.

Red: And what big eyes you have, gramma.

Wolf: All the better to see you with, my dear, heh-heh!

Red: And what a big nose you have, gramma.

Wolf: All the better to smell your goodies with, my dearie.

Red: And what big teeth you have gramma.

Wolf: (jumps up out from the blanket) Yeah! All the better to eat you with . . .!

> Red Riding Hood pulls the gun out of the basket and shoots about six shots in to the wolf.

Wolf: (staggers, falls to his knees) Well, folks, the moral of this story is . . . "Little girls just ain't as dumb as they used to be." (falls)

THE MAD REPORTER

The scene is the Golden Gate Bridge. A very depressed newspaper reporter is about to jump. (The edge of a stage or platform can be used as the edge of the bridge.)

Characters:
1. Reporter
2. Woman
3. Teenager
4. Man

Reporter: I've had it. I'm through. I'm all washed up. I just can't get a big story. Two years on the newspaper staff and not a single big story. I'm going to jump off this bridge and end it all! (Starts to jump, but stops when lady enters . . .)

Woman: Life is terrible. My husband doesn't love me. My kids can't stand me. I'm a failure in everything I do. Even the women's liberation movement is against me. (Cries)

Reporter: Why don't you just jump off this bridge with me. I'm going to end it all.

Woman: You're right. Let's go. (Counting together) One . . . Two . . . (teenager enters)

Teenager: Life is really a drag. I just can't go on this way. What do I have to look forward to? Nothing. Overpopulation. Pollution. Wars. Poverty. We can send men to the moon, but I can't find a job. I've had it . . .

Reporter: Excuse me, but I couldn't help but overhearing. We are going to end it all by jumping off the bridge here. Why don't you join us?

Teenager: Gladly.

All: One . . . Two . . . Three . . . (stops when man enters)

Man: What am I going to do? The stock market left me broke. My wife has run away with the milkman. I lost my job. My house burned down. Nothing but re-runs on television . . .

Reporter: Hey, mister. We're going to end it all right now. It's the easiest way out.

Man: Good idea.

All: One . . . Two . . . Three . . . JUMP! (They all jump except the reporter).

Reporter: Wow! What a story! Three people jump to their death! I can see it now on the front page! Wait til the boss sees this! (Exits)

THE MAGIC BANDANA

For this skit, you will need two guys. One is a magician, the other is his assistant. The magician should be dressed appropriately in tails, top hat, etc. and the assistant should appear to be somewhat of a clutz. He (the assistant) never says anything, a la Harpo Marx. He only takes orders from his "boss," the magician. On the stage is a table. On top of the table is a bandana (a red handkerchief). Also, nearby (like under the table) is a sack lunch.

Magician: Ladies and gentlemen, today I am going to perform for you my famous vanishing bandana trick. My assistant, Herkimer, will go to the table behind me, and do exactly as I say. And even though I will not look at Herkimer or the bandana, I will be able to make it disappear in Herkimer's hand. (To Herkimer) All right, Herkimer . . . go to the table behind me. (Herkimer goes to the table, and the magician stands in front, facing the audience, so that he cannot see the table or Herkimer.)

Magician: Herkimer . . . please pick up the bandana. (Herkimer looks at the bandana, but is distracted by the sack lunch under the table, so he picks it up and looks inside the bag. He discovers a banana. Then he looks puzzled, like he's not sure exactly what the magician asked him to pick up, so he throws the bandana on the floor, and holds the banana instead.)

Magician: Herkimer . . . Take the bandana in your right hand, please. (He holds the banana in his right hand.)

Magician: Now, Herkimer . . . fold the four corners of the bandana together. (Herkimer begins peeling the banana, counting one, two, three, four. Then he throws the peel on the floor.)

Magician: Now, Herkimer . . . fold the bandana in half. (Herkimer folds the banana in half.)

Magician: Now stuff the bandana into your left fist and don't let any of it show, Herkimer . . . (Herkimer takes the banana and crams it into his fist, causing the squashed up banana to come oozing out between his fingers.)

Magician: Finally, Herkimer . . . on the count of three . . . throw the bandana up into the air, and the bandana will be gone! ONE . . . TWO . . . (On the count of three, Herkimer throws the mashed up banana at the magician . . . and the magician chases Herkimer off stage.)

THE MIDGET SKIT

This hilarious skit requires two people who are reasonably creative. It works best when presented on a stage with a curtain and no lighting except for a spotlight on the "midget." You will need the following props:

1. Table covered with a sheet or blanket.
2. Men's long sleeved shirt
3. Bermuda shorts
4. Shoes (large work shoes are best)
5. Paper bag containing one toothbrush, can of shaving cream, safety razor (no blade in it), banana, peanut butter and jam sandwich, cream pie.
6. Towel lying on table.

The lead man of this skit should be someone who can ad-lib reasonably well. He stands behind the table with his hands in the shoes. A helper stands directly behind him and puts his hands through the sleeves of the shirt. The shorts go around the lead man's arms.

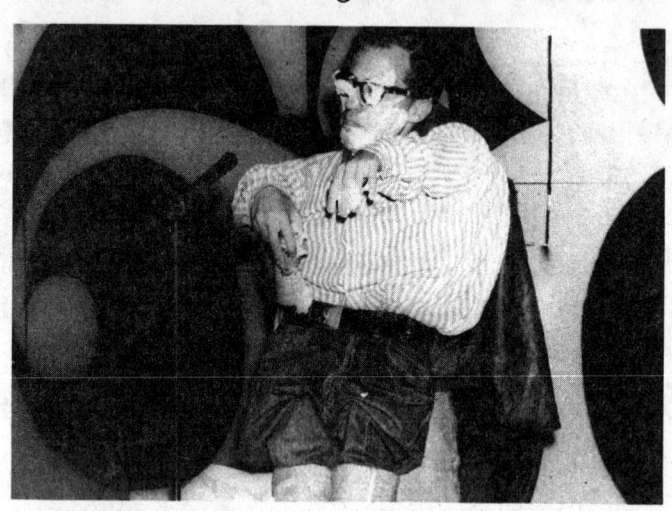

During the course of the skit it will be necessary for the "midget" to shave, brush his teeth, eat, etc. The arms will be doing all the activity and of course the arms can't see what they're doing. The movement should all be exaggerated by smearing toothpaste all over the lead man's nose, brushing his cheeks, sticking a banana in his eye, etc. The feet can also do some funny things by clicking heels together, running, etc.

The lead man's monologue can be hilarious. One good idea is to have the "midget" hitch-hiking to some event (that you want to advertise). Explain to the audience that you are going to a certain place and need a ride. Several cars go by. Finally, one stops and the "midget" gets in (although he does not actually move anywhere). He talks to the driver of the car and explains where he is going and asks if he can shave before he gets there. He does and then asks if he can eat his lunch. After he eats his lunch he brushes his teeth, gets out of the car and thanks the driver. The "midget" can also be a girl. You can either change the costuming or use two girls and then supply beauty aids such as lipstick, mascara, etc. Then have a beauty class. The more creative and uninhibited the participants are, the more successful the skit will be.

MOTHER, I'M DYING!

Director: Tonight the Little Theatre Guild would like to present a new avant-garde play about a provocative teenage tragedy. The characters are the daughter, the mother, the doctor, the mortician. Our scene opens with mother sitting in the living room as the teenage daughter enters with a problem.

NOTE: The following scene is acted without any emotion and completely deadpan.

Daughter: Mother, I think I'm dying.

Mother: Oh, thank goodness it's nothing serious. I suppose I should call the doctor. I hate to inconvenience him. (crosses to phone) Hello, doctor. Oh, I'm fine, thank you. How are you? Say, my daughter says she thinks she's dying. When you get time, could you come over and check on her.

The daughter lays down on a table. There is a knock at the door and mother gets up to answer.

Mother: Oh, hello, doctor. Come on in. My daughter's collapsed over there. Would you like some coffee? (he politely refuses)

Doctor: (Bends over the daughter and listens with stethoscope) Why your daughter's not dying . . . she's dead.

Mother: Well, how about that. Guess I'll call the mortician. (crosses to phone) Hello, mortician. Say, my daughter's dead, do you think you could come over within a few days and take care of her? OK. Goodbye.

The mortician knocks at the door and the mother answers.

Mother: Hello, mortician, my daughter's over there.

Mortician: (Measures daughter from head to toe) She'll fit.

Director: (Furious) Stop! Stop! That was terrible! That was the worst acting I've ever seen. Where was the emotion? There wasn't any! None! Now, I want you to do the whole thing over again. This time use a little emotion . . . in fact, use a lot of emotion!!!

The cast repeats the entire skit this time crying hysterically. Every actor delivers their lines sobbing and wailing uncontrollably. The lines do not have to be delivered exactly because the audience will respond to the crying. Of course, the more creative and uninhibited the actors the better. When the skit ends this time the director again jumps to his feet and shouts:

Director: That was horrible! What's the matter with you knuckleheads? Now you went too far with the emotion. You can't have all tears and sadness. Now, do it over again. This time use some humor. After all, even Shakespeare had humor in his tragedies.

The cast repeats the complete skit over this time laughing hysterically. When the skit is over then the director jumps up and throws them out.

THE NEWLYWEDS

The scene is the breakfast table of a newly married couple. Two people are required. For added laughs, use two guys, with one dressed up like a girl.

She: Darling?

He: Yes, dear?

She: Isn't it wonderful being married?

He: Sure is, Sweetheart.

She: Honey, I was just wondering something . . .

He: Yes, Sugar-plum what's that?

She: Well, seeing as how we've been married only a few short hours and everything, I was just wondering if, before breakfast, you would come over here and give me a little kiss on the cheek . . . (giggle)

He: (embarrassed) In broad daylight? Aw Shucks . . .

She: Please?? Just a little peck on the cheek right here (points to a place on her cheek)

He: We'lllll . . . O.K. (He kisses her on the cheek)

She: Ahhhhh. Good! I've been trying to pop that zit for a week!!

One-Liners

The following skits are very short "one-liners" that can be used many different ways. In some cases, the "punch line" is funny enough to carry the skit, but in most cases, the real humor is in the acting out of the skit by the participants. Timing and execution is very important in skits as these.

It is suggested that you select a number of these skits (twenty or so) and present them all at once "shotgun" style, that is, one right after another. There should be no pause between them at all. Simply have the necessary props out on the stage area ahead of time for all the skits, and then have the kids put them on with as much gusto as possible. You may use a small number of kids, and have them switch costumes back and forth, acting out many different parts. Sometimes it is helpful to have a lively musical interlude between each skit, such as old time piano music, or a vaudeville-type fanfare. Use your imagination, creativity, and the result will be a lot of fun for everyone.

THE HOLDUP

Man: Say, buddy, do you see any cops around?

Stranger: No.

Man: Okay, then stick-em-up!

THE BEAUTY SHOP

Smith: My wife spent four hours in the beauty shop this morning!

Jones: That's a long time.

Smith: You're not kidding. And that was just for the ESTIMATE!

THE HAT

Lady: My husband says I look younger in this hat

Friend: Oh really? How old are you?

Lady: Thirty.

Friend: No, I mean, *without* the hat . . .

THE DREAM

Wife: Dear, I dreamed you gave me a hundred dollars for new clothes last night. You wouldn't want to spoil that nice dream, now, would you???

Husband: Of course not, dear. You can keep the money.

THE SANDWICH SHOP

Customer: Waiter, the sign outside says that you will pay $50.00 to anyone who can order a sandwich that you don't have. Okay, I'd like an *elephant ear* sandwich!

Waiter: Oh-Oh. I guess we'll have to pay you the 50 bucks.

Customer: No elephant ears, eh? (smiling)

Waiter: Nah, we've got lots of them. We're just out of those *big buns.*

AT THE DOOR

Visitor: Was that your wife who met me at the door and took my hat and coat?

Man: You don't think I'd hire a maid that ugly, do you?

THE HANGMAN

Hangman: (As he places the noose around the criminal's neck) You'll have to excuse me if I seem a little nervous. You see, this is my first hanging.

Criminal: Mine, too.

THE ROPE

Observer: Say, what are you pulling that rope for?

Man: Have you ever tried to push one of these things?

THE WIRE

Messenger: Wire for Mr. Jones! Wire for Mr. Jones!

Jones: I'm Mr. Jones

Messenger: Here you are, sir. (Hands him a piece of wire)

THE ESKIMOS

One Eskimo: I saw someone kissing your wife last night.

Other Eskimo: Yeah, well, that's no skin off my nose.

THE REVEREND AND THE GOLF BALL

Man: Reverend, I'm really sorry that I swore like that. That's what I like about you. When your ball goes in the rough you never swear.

Reverend: That may be . . . but when I spit, the grass dies!

THE MEDICINE

Lady: The doctor told me to take this medicine after a hot bath.

Friend: Did you take it?

Lady: No. I could hardly finish drinking the hot bath.

THE HAMBURGER

Customer: Hey waiter, there's a hair in my hamburger!

Waiter: (yells to the cook, offstage) Hey, Smitty! Could you come out here a minute? This fellow's got a problem with his hamburger!

Cook: (Comes out with no shirt on, only hat and apron) I'll be there as soon as I finish making these hamburger patties. (He rolls up meat and mashes it down under his armpit.)

THE MIND READER

Mindreader: Would you like your palm read?

Customer: Yes.

Mindreader: (Takes out red paint, and paints his hand.)

ON THE AIRLINER

Stewardess: Sir, I think we left your wife behind in Chicago!

Man: Oh, thank goodness. I thought I was going deaf.

THE COED

Girl: I went away to college to find Mr. Perfect, but when I got there I found out that I wasn't the only pebble on the beach.

Friend: What did you do?

Girl: I became a little boulder.

THE TIE

Man: Say, that's a beautiful rainbow tie that you're wearing.

Other man: What do you mean, *rainbow* tie?

Man: It has a big POT at the end.

THE BUS RIDE

Lady: Sir, are you enjoying your bus ride?

Man: Yes, ma'am.

Lady: Then why are you sitting there with your eyes shut? Are you sick?

Man: No, I'm okay. It's just that I hate to see a woman stand.

HAND ME DOWNS

Smith: We were so poor that when I was a kid, I had to wear "hand-me-downs"!

Jones: That's not so bad. Everybody has to wear hand-me-downs.

Smith: But all I had were older sisters!

THE SINGER

Singer: (Using a strainer for a microphone) "Some-where . . . over the Rainbow . . ."

Man: Hey, don't do that!

Singer: (Stops singing) Why?

Man: You'll strain your voice.

THE POOR MAN

Poor man: My family was really poor.

Friend: How do you know they were so poor?

Poor man: That's easy. Everytime I passed someone in town, they would say, there goes Bobby Jones. His *poor* family. . .

UGLY BABY

Passenger: Lady, that is the ugliest baby I've ever seen!

Lady: (Starts crying.)

Busdriver: (Stops bus) What's the problem, ma'am? Here, use my handkerchief, and . . . here's a banana for your little monkey.

TOPLESS RESTAURANT

Customer: Wow, I've never been in a topless restaurant before! (Starts drinking his water)

Waiter: (Big guy comes out without his shirt on, hairy chest and all.)

Customer: (Spits out water.)

THE GALLOWS

Man: Say, what are you guys doing!!!

Bully: We're hanging this man! In this town, we hang all murderers and all sissies!

Man: (in a real deep voice) OH, REALLY?

IN THE OFFICE

Employee: Say, boss, since your assistant died, I was wondering if maybe I could take his place . . .

Employer: It's all right with me if you can arrange it with the undertaker.

THE PASTOR

Member: Pastor, how did you get that cut on your face?

Pastor: I was thinking about my sermon this morning, and wasn't concentrating on what I was doing . . . and I cut myself while shaving.

Member: That's too bad. Next time, you had better concentrate on your shaving and cut your sermon!

THE NEW HAT

Husband: Where did you get that new hat?

Wife: Don't worry, dear. It didn't cost a thing. It was marked down from $20 to $10. So I bought it with the $10 that I saved.

CROSSED UP

Smith: Know what happened when they crossed an abalone with a crocodile?

Jones: No, what?

Smith: A "Crock-a-baloney."

THE FRESH GUY

Girl: When I went out with Pete, I had to slap his face five times.

Friend: Was he that fresh?

Girl: No. I thought he was dead.

THE TEACHER

Girl: Did you kiss me when the lights went out?

Boy: No!

Girl: It must have been that fellow over there.

Boy: Why, I'll teach him a thing or two!!!

Girl: You couldn't teach him a thing!

THE PIE

Man: Waitress, what kind of pie is this that I'm eating?

Waitress: Well, what does it taste like?

Man: It tastes like fish.

Waitress: Oh, that must be the lemon pie. The apple pie tastes like garlic.

THE PIZZA

Cook: Say, mister. Do you want me to cut this pizza into six or eight pieces?

Man: You better make it six. I don't think I can eat eight.

THE GORILLA

Smith: Know what they got when they crossed a gorilla with a porcupine?

Jones: No, what?

Smith: I don't know what they call it, but it sure gets a seat on the subway.

WHALE SANDWICH

Man: Say, waiter. Your sign outside says, "Any sandwich you can name." O.K. I want a WHALE sandwich!

Waiter: One whale sandwich coming up. (Leaves, goes into kitchen and comes out again.) Sorry. I can't get you a whale sandwich.

Man: Why not? Your sign says "ANY SANDWICH!"

Waiter: Well, the cook says he doesn't want to start a new whale for one lousy sandwich.

THE SERVICE

Man: Isn't this a beautiful church. Look . . . here's a plaque on the wall dedicated to all the brave men who died in the service.

Lady: Which one . . . Morning or Evening?

MOUNTAIN LION

Smith: Know what they got when they crossed a mountain lion and a parrot?

Jones: No, what?

Smith: I don't know what they call it, but when it talks, you listen!

BULLFIGHTER

Man: Did you hear about the bullfighter that became a fireman?

Other man: No. What about him?

Man: Well, he went to a fire and some guy jumped out of a three story window into his net.

Other man: Then what happened?

Man: He went "O-LAY!" (Moves net like in bullfight)

SNAKE BITE

Smith: Know what they got when they crossed a rattlesnake with a horse?

Jones: No, what?

Smith: I don't know what they call it, but if it bites you, you can ride it to the hospital.

FLOWER DISEASE

Girl: He's got the awful "flower disease"!

Other girl: What's that?

Girl: He's a blooming idiot!

THE CANARY

Man: Know what the 500 pound canary said?

Other man: No, what?

Man: (deep voice) CHERP!

THE BANQUET

Speaker: This is terrible. I am the speaker at this banquet and I forgot to bring my false teeth with me.

Man: I happen to have an extra pair. Try these.

Speaker: Too small.

Man: Well, try this pair.

Speaker: Too big.

Man: Well, I have one more pair . . . how about these?

Speaker: These fit just fine. Boy, I sure am lucky to be sitting next to a dentist.

Man: I'm not a dentist. I'm an undertaker.

DIET SHAMPOO

Girl: Have you tried that new DIET shampoo?

Boy: No.

Girl: Well you should. It's for FATHEADS.

CHRISTMAS GIFT

Smith: What did you give your wife for Christmas last year?

Jones: A cemetery plot.

Smith: What are you going to give her this year?

Jones: Nothing. She didn't use last year's gift.

THE GET WELL CARD

Man: How are you feeling, pastor?

Pastor: Much better, thank you.

Man: Well, we had a committee meeting the other night and they voted to send you this get-well card. The motion passed four to three.

DON'T WORRY

Man: You shouldn't worry like that. It doesn't do any good.

Other man: It does for me! Ninety percent of the things that I worry about never happen!

THE NIBBLE

Old lady: Dear, when we were younger, you used to nibble on my

	ear.
Old man:	I'll be right back.
Old lady:	Where are you going?
Old man:	To get my teeth!

THE THREE WIVES

Man:	Did you hear about the guy who had three wives in three months? The first two died from eating poisoned mushrooms.
Friend:	What happened to the third?
Man:	She died from a blow on the head. She wouldn't eat the mushrooms.

THE COMPUTER

Inventor:	I've invented a computer that's almost human!
Man:	You mean it can think on its own?
Inventor:	No. But when it makes a mistake, it blames another computer!

THE DRESS

Woman:	This dress that I have on will never go out of style.
Other woman:	No it won't. It'll look just as ridiculous every year.

ELEPHANT PAJAMAS

Hunter:	One night in the jungle, I heard a noise outside my tent. I looked outside and an elephant was charging. I ran outside, grabbed my gun, and shot him *in my pajamas!*
Man:	That's ridiculous. How did he ever get into your pajamas?

FAMOUS MEN

Visitor:	Have any famous men ever been born in this town?
Native:	Nope. Just little babies.

EVERY TWENTY MINUTES

Man:	According to this report, a person is hit by an automobile every twenty minutes!
Other man:	What a glutton for punishment that guy must be!

WANT AD

Girl: My dog ran away last night.

Boy: Did you put an ad in the paper?

Girl: No.

Boy: Why not?

Girl: My dog can't read.

MUD PACKS

Man: Ever so often, my wife puts on one of those mud-packs.

Friend: Does it improve her looks?

Man: Yes, for a few days. Then the mud falls off.

THE OCEAN

Girl: You remind me of an ocean . . .

Boy: You mean . . . wild . . . restless . . . romantic . . .???

Girl: No. I mean you make me sick.

THE FISHERMAN

Man: Where are you going?

Fisherman: (mumbled) Fishing.

Man: What have you got in your mouth?

THE NEWSBOY

Newsboy: Extra! Extra! Read all about it! Two men swindled!

Man: I'll take one. (Looks at paper.) Hey, there's nothing here about two men being swindled!

Newsboy: Extra! Extra! THREE men swindled!

THE INHERITANCE

Girl: I think you only married me because my father left me a lot of money!

Husband: That's not true. I couldn't care less WHO left you the money!

THE PSYCHIATRIST

This is a skit that requires two persons: the psychiatrist and his patient. The scene is the doctor's office. The only props needed are a couch (for the patient to lie down on) and a chair for the doctor. The skit begins with a knock on the doctor's door, and he answers it.

Man: Oh, ah, hello there . . . are you Dr. Kaseltzer, the psychiatrist?

Doc: Yes I am, and that will be 20 dollars. What other questions can I help you with?

Man: Well, my name is Mr. Gaspocket . . . I have an appointment.

Doc: Oh yes, What's the nature of your problem?

Man: Well, I'm trying to break—bark!—a nervous habit.

Doc: Well, maybe I can help you.

Man: Thanks, doc.—bark!

Doc: How long has this been going on?

Man: Oh, ever since I was a teenager.—bark!

Doc: Hmmm . . . Think back. Were you ever frightened by a vicious dog?

Man: Huh? I don't get it.

Doc: Well, these problems can often be traced to some single event.

Man: No, this is just a—bark!—nervous habit.

Doc: Have you ever tried to break it before?

Man: Oh yes, I've tried lots of things, such as wearing gloves.

Doc: Wait a minute. You've tried wearing gloves?

Man: Yes. Well, you know, I thought if I would start wearing gloves, I might stop biting my nails.

Doc: Biting your nails?

Man: Well, yes. That's the nervous habit I was telling you about.

Doc: You mean you came to see me just because you bite your nails?

Man: Well, certainly. What else—bark!—what else in the world—bark!—would I have on my mind?

Doc: Maybe you should lie down here and tell me all about it.

Man: Well, I'm not allowed on the furniture.

Doc: That's all right, I don't mind.

Man: Well, all right. You see, one reason I get nervous and bite my nails is—bark!—because of my mother.

Doc: Your mother?

Man: Well, she always made me sleep on a bunch of newspapers down in the cellar. Somehow, she got this crazy quirk, you know, she got it in her mind, now you won't believe this, but she got to the point that she imagined that I went around the house, now listen to this, that I went around the house **barking** like a dog!

Doc: You think she imagined this?

Man: Well, I know she did, you know, she finally wrote to a doctor about me . . . a Veterinarian.

Doc: Oh really? And what did he say?

Man: I don't know. I never let the mailman near the house.—bark! bark!

Doc: This goes deeper than I thought. I'm going to try the word association test. I'll say a word and you say the first word that comes to your mind . . . **Table!**

Man: Chair.

Doc: Ball.

Man: Bat.

Doc: Flower.

Man: Rose.

Doc: Cat.

Man: Bark!

Doc: Dog Catcher.

Man: Bark! Bark! Bark!

Doc: I'll tell you what. This is going to require some consultation. Why don't you come in next Thursday?

Man: Oh, no, Doc, couldn't you make it another day? I don't want to miss "Lassie."

Doc: Okay. How about Sunday night around 6?

Man: Nope, that's (announce youth group).

Doc: Okay. Let's make it Monday. Good day, sir.

Man: (exits) Bark! Bark!

QUICKIE SKITS

The idea behind each of these is the same. A guy comes running into the room acting strange, and the leader responds. It is best to have the guy come in at a seemingly inappropriate time, such as interrupting you as you are making an announcement. Most of these will get groans rather than wild laughter, so be prepared.

1. It's running down my back! It's running down my back!
   What is?
   My spine.

2. It's all around me! It's all around me!
   What is?
   My belt.

3. I can't see! I can't see!
   Why not?
   My eyes are closed.

4. It's all over us! It's all over us!
   What is?
   The roof.

5. Woman the Lifeboats! We're sinking! Woman the Lifeboats!
   You mean "man" the lifeboats, don't you?
   Look, you fill your lifeboats, I'll fill mine . . .

6. (Guy walks in carrying a paper bag)
   What's in the bag?
   Milk.
   That's ridiculous. You don't put milk in a BAG.
   Why not? Cows do.

RINSE THE BLOOD OFF MY TOGA

The following skit is a take off on Julius Caesar. It is one of the real classic skits and should be carefully learned and rehearsed before presentation. Use your own creativity as to sets, props, costumes, etc. The dialogue will usually carry the skit without elaborate props. The Characters:

1. Flavius Maximus
2. Secretary
3. Brutus
4. Calpurnia
5. Senators (three or four will do)
6. Mark Antony
7. Claudius
8. Tiberius
9. Sargeant

The scene: Rome—44 B.C.

Flavius: (To audience) My name is Flavius Maximus. I'm a private Roman eye. My license number is IXIVLLCCDIXMB. Also comes in handy as an eye chart. Tonight, I'm going to tell you about the Julius Caesar caper. It all began during the Ides of March. I was in my office. I'd just sent another criminal to jail . . . Sutonius, the Gladiator. He'd been fixing fights at the Coliseum. Had a crooked lion that kept taking a dive. Anyway, as I was sitting there, my secretary walked in.

Secretary: Good morning, Flavius, here's the mail.

Flavius: Easy with those marble postcards. Break my table. Anything else, babe?

Secretary: Yeh. There's somebody outside to see you. Seems awfully excited about something.

Flavius: O.K. Show him in, doll.

Secretary: Would you come in, Sir?

Brutus: Thank you, Miss. You Flavius Maximus, private Roman eye?

Flavius: Yeh, What's on your mind?

Brutus: Are you positive we're alone?

Flavius: I'm positive we're alone.

Brutus: Well, who's that standing beside you?

Flavius: That's you, stupid. (to audience) I could see I was dealing with no ordinary man. This guy was a nut! O.K., what's on your mind?

Brutus: Flavius Maximus, a terrible thing has happened. It's the greatest crime in the history of Rome.

Flavius: Aw'right, give it to me straight. What's up?

Brutus: Julius Caesar has been murdered!

Flavius: (To audience) Julius Caesar murdered! I couldn't believe my ears! Big Juli was dead!

Brutus: Yeh, He was killed just 20 minutes ago. It happened in the Senate. He was stabbed.

Flavius: Stabbed?

Brutus: Yeh, They got him right in the rotunda!

Flavius: Oh, that's a painful spot. I had a splinter there once.

Brutus: Yeh.

Flavius: Those marble splinters, you know.

Brutus: Boy, I tell you, all of Rome is in an uproar. I came to you because you're the top private eye in Rome. You've got to find the killer.

Flavius: Well (ha, ho), I'll try.

Brutus: Aw, you can do it. After all, you're the guy who got Nero. You sent him up on that arson rap.

Flavius: Oh yeh, Nero. The whole town was sure burnt up about him, eh? (Ha, Ha, Ha) You get it? The whole town—Shades of Jupiter!

Brutus: Well, look. What do you say Flavius? Will you take the case?

Flavius: Just a minute, paly. I like to know who I'm working for. Just who are you?

Brutus: I'm a senator. I was Caesar's best friend. The name's Brutus.

Flavius: Brutus, eh? All right, Brutus, you got yourself a boy. I'll take the case. My fee is 125 dracmas a day—payable in advance.

Brutus: O.K. Here you are. (Sound of money)

Flavius: You're one short.

Brutus: Hey, you got a good ear.

Flavius: When it comes to money, perfect pitch. Let's go, eh? (To audience) We went outside, flagged a passing chariot, and made our way down the Via Appia. The streets were crowded with the usual people—slaves, legionnaires, patricians and little men who came out of doorways and sold you postcards from Gaul. Before long we found ourselves at the Senate. (Sounds of men in Senate)

Brutus: Well, Flavius, this is where it happened. This is where Big Juli got knocked off.

Flavius: Yeh, Now where's the corpus delicti?

Brutus: The what?

Flavius: The corpus delicti. What's a matter, don't you understand plain Latin? The body!

Brutus: Oh, the stiff.

Flavius: Yeh.

Brutus: Oh, he's laying right over there.

Flavius: Wowee! Eight daggers in him.

Brutus: Yeh, what do you think?

Flavius: If he were alive today he'd be a pretty sick boy!

Brutus: Yeh.

Flavius: He's really fixed for blades, eh? (Ha, Ha)

Brutus: Aw, come on, Flavius. You gotta solve this crime.

Flavius: Aw' right, aw' right. Fill me in on the set-up here. Now who are those guys over there?

Brutus: They were all here when it happened. That's Publius; that's Casca; there's Tribonius.

Flavius: I see. Who's that guy over there with the lean and hungry look on his kisser?

Brutus: That's Cassius.

Flavius: Yeh, looks like a loser from the Coliseum. Now, who do you think is the likeliest suspect?

Brutus: That fellow next to him.

Flavius: Wait a minute, that's you.

Brutus: I know, but can I be trusted?

Flavius: (To audience) I could see I was dealing with no ordinary case. This was a mental case. (Sound of walking) Wait a minute. Uh, who's the dame?

Brutus: Oh, 'that's Caesar's wife. Her name is Calpurnia.

Flavius: Yeh, well, she's a suspect.

Brutus: Sure.

Flavius: Just a minute, Pardon me. Uh—Mrs. Caesar?

Calpurnia: Yes?

Flavius: Flavius Maximus, private Roman eye. I'd like to ask you a few questions. What do you know about this?

Calpurnia: I told him. I told him, "Juli, don't go."

Flavius: Wha?

Calpurnia: "Juli, don't go," I told him. No, he wouldn't listen to me.

Flavius: Now look, Mrs. Caesar, I . . .

Calpurnia: If I told him once, I've told him a thousand times, "Juli don't go . . ."

Flavius: Now, please don't upset yourself . . .

Calpurnia: I begged him, don't go. I told him, "Juli, don't go." I said, "It's the Ides of March. Beware, already."

Flavius: Yeh . . .

Calpurnia: But would he listen to his wife? No!

Flavius: All right, take it easy! Sergeant, would you take Mrs. Caesar home, please.

Sergeant: Come along, ma'am. Come along.

Calpurnia: I told him, "Juli, don't go." (Fade out) I told him, "Juli, don't go."

Flavius: (I don't blame him for going!) All right, you senators. You can go too, but don't leave town.

Senators: (Mumble)

Brutus: Well, what do you think?

Flavius: I don't know! Not an angle anywhere. Not a clue.

Brutus: Well, cheer up, Flavius. After all, Rome wasn't built in a day.

Flavius: Say, ah . . . What was that?

Brutus: I said, "Rome wasn't built in a day."

Flavius: That's . . . that's very good. (Rome wasn't built in a day) That's **very** good.

Brutus: You like it?

Flavius: Yeh.

Brutus: It's yours.

Flavius: Thanks. Well, let's reconstruct the crime. Now, Caesar was

	over there and . . .
Brutus:	Right over here, yeh.
Flavius:	Hst.
Brutus:	What's the matter?
Flavius:	Somebody is behind that pillar. I'll go get him. Hsh. (pause) All right buddy. Come on. Come on out. What are you doing here?
Mark:	(Cries of agony) Stop it.
Flavius:	All right, buster. What are you doin' hangin' around here?
Mark:	Well, why shouldn't I? I'm Mark Antony.
Flavius:	Mark Antony?
Mark:	Yeh, I just made a speech over the body of Caesar. I said, "Friends, Romans, Countrymen, lend me your ears!"
Flavius:	Yeh? What you got in that sack?
Mark:	Ears!
Flavius:	Will you get out of here!
Mark:	Wait a minute. Don't you want to know who bumped off Julius Caesar?
Flavius:	Yeh. You know who did it? Out with it. What's his name?
Mark:	His name is ahh—oooooo—eeeee—ohhhhh—ahhhhh.
Flavius:	That's a funny name. Must be Greek.
Brutus:	No. Look! He's dead.
Flavius:	(To audience) What a confusing case. All I got for clues is two dead bodies and a sackful of ears.
Brutus:	Now, look. Flavius. I'm paying you 100 dracmas a day.
Flavius:	125 dracmas.
Brutus:	All right, you got a good ear.
Flavius:	I got a **sackful** of good ears.
Brutus:	Now look—look. Let's have some action here, eh?
Flavius:	All right, all right. Don't get your toga in a knot. Listen, I got a pal.
Brutus:	Yeh?
Flavius:	Claudius. Runs a bar on the Via Flaminia. He should have a few answers for me.

Brutus: Hey, that's the idea. Get out among the people, ask questions. After all, when in Rome, do as the Romans do.

Flavius: Hey, uh . . . what was that one? What was that one?

Brutus: I said, "When in Rome, do as the Romans do."

Flavius: Oh . . . that's . . . that's very good. "When in Rome, do as the Romans do."

Brutus: You like it?

Flavius: Yeh.

Brutus: It's yours.

Flavius: Thanks. I'll see you later.

Brutus: All right. See ya!

Flavius: Claudius' bar and grill is a hangout where I get all the answers. It's just a small place with a few tables and a guy in the corner playing a cool reed pipe.

Claudius: Hi ya Flav.

Flavius: Hi Claud. What's new?

Claudius: Nothing much. What ya drinkin?

Flavius: Give me a martinus.

Claudius: You mean a Martini.

Flavius: If I want two, I'll ask for 'em. Look, I'm working on this Julius Caesar kill. You know anything?

Claudius: Try that dame over there.

Flavius: Yeh?

Claudius: Yeh.

Flavius: All right sister, start talkin'.

Calpurna: I told him, "Juli, don't go!"

Flavius: Oh no!

Calpurnia: "Juli, don't go . . ."

Flavius: Out! Out! Hsheeee!

Claudius: Hey, look, uh . . . Flavius. I, uh, think I know the guy you're looking for.

Flavius: You mean . . . Mr. Big?

Claudius: Yeh. His name is oooooo—eeeeeee—aaaaaaaa—eeeeeeeeeeg.

Flavius: Now that's an interesting name. Got a chisel? I'd like to write that down. Claudius! Claudius! (To audience) I would never get any more conversation from him. He was dead. This was shaping up bigger than I thought. Suddenly I looked up. There was Brutus.

Brutus: Hello, Flavius.

Flavius: Brutus, what are you doing here?

Brutus: Hey, I was lookin' for ya. Who's that there on the floor?

Flavius: Claudius, the bartender.

Brutus: Hey, that's a funny place for him to carry a knife . . . in his back.

Flavius: He's dead. He was stabbed—through the portico.

Brutus: Hey, that's even more painful than the rotunda.

Flavius: Yeh.

Brutus: Well, have you come up with any answers? Who killed Julius Caesar?

Flavius: (To audience) I started to think, and slowly the pieces fell into place. Brutus was the only man around when all those guys got killed—Caesar, Anthony, the bartender—Brutus was always there. Things were beginning to add up. I put two and two together and it came out IV. It was time to make my move . . .!

Brutus: What do you mean—IV?

Flavius: Four, stupid.

Brutus: Well, have you come up with any answers? Who killed Julius Caesar?

Flavius: Only one guy coulda done it.

Brutus: Yeh? Who?

Flavius: Let's not play games, Brutus . . . or should I say . . . Mr. Big!

Brutus: What are you gettin' at?

Flavius: If the Sandal fits, wear it. You knocked off Big Juli!

Brutus: Ha, Ha. You're out of your head. I hired you to find the killer.

Flavius: Pretty smart, but not smart enough! Now all right . . . You gonna talk, or do I have to call in a couple of centurions to lean on ya?

Brutus: All right, flatfoot. I did it. I admit it. I knocked off Big Juli, and I'd do it again.

Flavius: That's all I want to know. I'm sending you up the Tiber for a long stretch. Come on, I'll call a chariot, and we'll go downtown.

Brutus: Don't move unless you want a dagger in the toga.

Flavius: What?

Brutus: I'm gettin' out of here. Don't try to stop me!

Flavius: (To audience) He had the drop on me and I couldn't stop him, but I knew where he was heading. For the scene of the crime . . . the Senate. And 15 minutes later I pulled up in my chariot . . . Tiberius! Tiberius, hand me the ram's horn . . .

Tiberius: Here you are, Flav.

Flavius: (cups hands over mouth) All right Brutus. This is Flavius Maximus. I know you're in there. Now, come on out with your hands up!

Brutus: Hang it on your nose, you dirty rotten flatfoot! Come in and get me!

Flavius: Get smart, Brutus, we can smoke you out. We'll throw incense. We'll throw in an onion on a spear!

Brutus: I don't care what you do!

Flavius: All right, you asked for it! Give it to him. Tiberius! (Sound of breaking glass . . . Yelling and talking) All, Brutus, one false move and I'll fill ya full of bronze!

Brutus: All right, you got me, you creep. But I'll be back!

Flavius: Oh no you won't. This isn't a series.

Brutus: What?

Flavius: It's just one little Halloween party.

Brutus: Don't worry, I'll be back. Just remember one thing. "All roads lead to Rome."

Sergeant: Come on, you.

Flavius: Hey, wait, wait, wait, wait I bring him back!

Brutus: Huh . . . wat?

Flavius: Wait. Now that one was a dandy!

Brutus: What are you talking about?

Flavius: "All roads lead to Rome." That's the best, you know that?

Brutus: Do you like it?

Flavius: Yeh.

Brutus: Well, you can't have it.

Flavius: Oh, get out of here!

Man: Good work, Flavius. All Rome salutes you. Hail, Flavius!!!

All: Hail, Flavius!

Flavius: Thanks, boys . . . And now if you don't mind, I've got a date with a doll. O.K. Baby, I'm ready. Now you're sure your husband doesn't object?

Girl: Frankly, I don't care. I told him, "Juli, don't go . . ."

Flavius: Oh, no.

Girl: "Juli, don't go," I told him . . . (fade out)

THE SKYDIVER

This is an "interview" skit that requires two persons: a "roving reporter" and the skydiver, Rusty Ripcord. . . .

Announcer: Ladies and Gentlemen, this is your roving reporter here at Tonapah. Nevada, covering the world skydiving championships, for ABC's Weird World of Sports. Any moment now, the world's leading skydiver, Rusty Ripcord, will be along . . . (Enter Rusty all dressed up in a ridiculous outfit, goggles, rope, pack on back, inner tube, pump, combat boots, medals, helmet, tree limb, etc.)

Rusty: Boy, was that last jump a lulu!

Announcer: Excuse me, sir, Mr. Ripcord, how was your landing?

Rusty: Well, actually, not so hot . . . (pulls tree limb out of his clothes and tosses it down).

Announcer: Rusty, just how many jumps have you made?

Rusty: 95!

Announcer: Has your chute ever failed to open?

Rusty: Well yes, actually . . . 95 times.

Announcer: Wow, that must be rough!

Rusty: Not after the 1st time. . . .

Announcer: Say, I can't help but admiring your crash helmet you've got there. . . .

Rusty: Thanks. I got it with Raleigh Coupons. I also got my pants, my car, my house, my wife. . . .

Announcer: (interrupting) Say, what's that medal for?

Rusty: Oh that's when I won the First Invitational Indoor Skydiving Championship.

Announcer: Really? What are all those other medals for?

Rusty: Well, this one's for 27th place in the Girl Scout National Championship, and this one is for 49th place, Boys Five and under.

Announcer: What about this one? (points)

Rusty: Oh that holds my pants up.

Announcer: Is this your usual attire?

Rusty: Well, yeah, but its a little flat right now. (Pointing to inner tube around waist.)

Announcer: Rusty, what is your specialty?

Rusty: I specialize in diving over great bodies of water.

Announcer: Wow, that's terrific. Are there any specialty hazards?

Rusty: Yeah, I can't swim.

Announcer: What do you use that inner tube for?

Rusty: Well, it does come in handy as a life raft.

Announcer: Apparently so! How do you inflate it?

Rusty: Oh I just use this tire pump here.

Announcer: Really? How do you hold that pump on top of the water?

Rusty: (tries to demonstrate, but just gets tangled up. . . .)

Announcer: Rusty, I've heard that most skydivers yell "Geronimo!" when they jump. What do you yell?

Rusty: MOMMY!!!

Announcer: Rusty, when is the best time of the year to go skydiving?

Rusty: Anytime but fall.

Announcer: Why not fall?

Rusty: Birds flying South (Wipes eye . . .)

Announcer: Rusty, would you recommend skydiving to anyone in our viewing audience?

Rusty: Skydiving . . . It's the **OOONLY** way to fly!

Announcer: And now, back to our studios . . .

THE SPONTANEOUS MELODRAMA

This skit requires no preparation, except for collecting a few appropriate costumes. It is best with larger groups, and may be used with any age group, although it is best with older youth (high school on up). It requires nine participants (plus the narrator) who are chosen right out of the audience. They have no lines to read or to memorize. All they have to do is act out the story as it is read by the narrator When you select volunteers, try to choose people who are uninhibited and willing to give it their best shot. Also try to match the right kind of personalities with the parts required.

Characters Needed:
1. The Hero, Dudley DoRight
2. The Heroine, Prudence PureHeart
3. The Villain, Dirty Dan
4. Grandmother
5. The Dog (a boy who gets down on all fours)
6. The Cat (a girl who does the same)
7. The Chair (a boy on his hands and knees)
8. The Table (two boys, side by side on their hands and knees)

After the characters are chosen from the audience, have an assistant take them all "backstage" and dress them up in the costumes below.

Costume Suggestions: (Be creative! The more ridiculous, the better.)
1. Dudley: White boots, lipstick, Mickey Mouse Hat
2. Prudence: Long Blonde Wig (and a skirt, if you use a guy for this part)
3. Villain: Black cape, mustache, top hat
4. Grandmother: Gray wig, shawl, glasses

As soon as the actors are ready, the narrator begins reading the script. The audience are instructed to boo the villain, cheer for the hero, etc. The narrator should take his time through the script, reading with feeling, and pausing in the appropriate places to allow time for the actors to act. To give the actors more "incentive" to act with gusto, you might inform them that the audience will vote for "best actor" at the conclusion.

The Narrator reads the following script:

As our story opens, we find ourselves in a densely wooded forest where lovely PRUDENCE PUREHEART is picking wild blackberries while whistling a merry tune. (Pause while Prudence whistles, etc.) Unbeknownst to her, the village villain, DIRTY DAN, is creeping up behind her.
He grabs her and tries to steal a kiss!
She screams loud and long.
The villain covers her mouth with his hand as she screams.
She slaps the villain in the face.
He picks her up over his shoulder and carries her.
She screams and beats him.
He marches around in a circle three times, then heads for home to steal her Grandmother's money.
They exit.

MEANWHILE...

Back at the ranch Prudence's grandmother is sitting on a chair stirring some cake batter on the table.
The cat is sleeping underneath the table.
The old dog, Shep, enters the house and barks at the cat.
The cat jumps into Grandma's lap.
Grandmother slaps the cat and says, "Get down, you dirty creature."
The cat jumps down and runs outside.
The dog comes over and licks Grandma's hand.
He keeps licking her hand all the way up to the elbow.
Grandma kicks the dog.
The dog goes and lies in the corner.

Just then, the villain enters the room with Prudence on his shoulder.
Grandmother screams.
The villain says, "I am taking Prudence and your money."
The dog rushes over and bites the villain on the leg.
The villain kicks the dog and lets Prudence down.
Prudence faints onto the floor.
The dog barks at the villain, then goes over and starts licking Prudence's face to revive her.
He licks her face for 15 seconds while she remains perfectly still.
Just then, our hero. Dudley DoRight enters and shouts. "Forsooth and anon!"
Prudence stands up and screams, "Oh, my darling Dudley!"
Dudley and Prudence embrace.
Dudley says, "I love you, my precious."
Prudence says, "I love you my little lotus blossom."
All of a sudden the villain picks up the chair and throws it at Dudley.
It knocks Dudley down to the floor.
Prudence faints and falls onto the table.
Grandmother tries to revive her by slapping her hand, while sobbing, "My child, my child." This goes on and on . . .
The cat re-enters the house, jumps on the chair and runs underneath the table.
Dudley stands up and begins flexing his muscles.
The villain begins to tremble and shake and his knees knock together. This goes on and on. The dog starts barking and the cat starts meowing and this goes on and on.
Dudley decides to warm up for the fight so he does a few exercises by starting out with 10 jumping jacks. Then he runs in place for 15 seconds.
All this while Grandmother is sobbing and slapping, the villain is trembling, the dog is barking and the cat is meowing.
Then Dudley does 15 pushups.
On the 15th pushup, the villain seizes his opportunity and hits Dudley on the head.
Dudley falls to the floor, unconscious.
Just then the cat scratches the dog's nose.
The dog and cat have fight right on the top of Dudley for 10 seconds.
Then the dog chases the cat outside. Just then the table collapses under Prudence's weight and falls to the ground . . . table, Prudence, Grandmother, and all.
Prudence remains unconscious.
Granny shouts, "You nasty villain!" and starts hitting him in the stomach.
The villain doubles over.
Granny then goes around and kicks him in the seat.
The villain straightens up.
She hits him some more in the stomach over and over.

The villain again bends over.
She gives him a rabbit punch on the back of the neck.
He collapses unconscious to the floor.
Granny looks around at the three unconscious bodies.
She then straightens her shawl around her head and heads for the door for a night on the town saying, "All's well that ends well!"
(Contributed by Larry Wiens; Fresno, California)

THE STAND IN SKIT

Characters:
1. Director (wearing a beret, scarf, dark glasses, etc.)
2. Camera Man (with a "movie camera" of some kind. Try using an old fashioned meat grinder on a tripod to look like a camera.)
3. Make Up Man (with a sack of flour and a powder puff)
4. The Hero (handsome, dressed in white)
5. The beautiful girl
6. Bartender (or soda jerk . . .)
7. The sucker (the stand-in)

The skit begins with an apparent movie making set-up. The hero is sitting in a chair. next to the girl, getting ready to kiss her, and the camera man is moving around taking pictures, the director is directing the action, lights are on, etc. The "sucker," who is the dumb type, walks into the action, apparently intrigued with the whole thing, as he has never seen a real movie set before. He walks in front of the "camera" and interrupts the action.

Sucker: Wow. A real movie. Gosh I wish I could be in a movie.

Director: (in a rage) CUT! CUT! You! Get out of here! You've just ruined a perfect take! Beat it! Scram!

Sucker: (runs off, disappointed) Shucks. I shore wish I could be a movie star.

Director: (thinks a second) Hey, Wait a minute! You! (to the sucker) Do you want to be in a movie? I think we can use you! (He whispers to the hero something, and they both smile.)

Sucker: (overjoyed) Really? Wow! I'm a star! Oh boy! Where do I start? Where are my lines? . . .

Director: Just wait and we'll show you.

The action continues, and the hero sits again by the girl, says a bunch of mushy things to her, and then starts to kiss her. When he does, the girl brings back her hand to slap the hero's face . . .

Director: Cut! O.K., bring in the stand-in! (the sucker takes the place of the hero in the chair.) Make-up! (the make-up man comes in and throws a bunch of flour in the sucker's face.) Action!!

The sucker starts to kiss the girl, and she slaps him across the face so hard that he falls clean over backwards in his chair.

Director: Cut! Great! All right, let's have scene two! . . . Action !!!

The hero crawls along the floor, crying "Water, Water, Give me some water . . ."

Director: Cut! Bring in the stand-in! (He comes in and takes the hero's place) Make-up!! (Make-up man throws more flour in his face.) Action! Roll-em!

The sucker crawls along the ground and yells "Water." An off-stage helper brings in a big bucket of water and dumps it all over him.

Director: Cut! Perfect! All right, let's have scene three! . . . Action!

The hero walks up to a bar and orders some milk. The bartender gives him some milk and he drinks it. Then he orders some pie. The bartender says, "Do you **really** want some pie?" The hero says, "Yeah. Gimme some pie." The bartender reaches for some pie . . .

Director: Cut! Bring in the stand-in! . . . (the sucker enters, looking pretty bewildered at the whole thing) . . . Make-up! . . . (more flour in the face) . . . Action!

The sucker stands at the bar, demands the pie, and the bartender throws the pie (big cream pie) in his face.

Director: Cut! . . . Perfect! Tremendous! . . . Well, that's it for today!

Everybody leaves, leaving the stand-in with a puzzled look on his face. He shrugs his shoulders and walks off the stage.

TADPOLES SKIT

For this skit you need two inexpensive guitars that can be broken up, but are playable. Two guys are needed, one who can play the guitar. (It is best if these guys are the group leaders, such as the youth director or sponsors.) They are introduced to the group as the new folk-singing group, the TADPOLES! The two guys enter with guitars and begin to sing a folk song, such as "Tom Dooley" or any folk song and the following occurs:

1. Guy #1 (Bob) starts singing off key, annoying guy #2 (Mike). Mike insults Bob for his singing and with his finger snaps a string on Bob's guitar, by pulling it and letting go.
2. Mike starts singing and Bob stops him, takes out a pair of wire-cutters and snips all of Bob's strings except one.
3. Bob starts singing again, and Mike stops him, takes his guitar

away, picks up a saw and saws the neck of Bob's guitar off, and hands it back to him.
4. Bob then puts his guitar down, walks over and turns Mike's guitar over, with the back of the guitar facing the audience. (Mike holding it.) Bob sticks a target on the back of the guitar, and picks up a hammer and smashes a big hole in it.
5. Mike then takes Bob's guitar and puts it on the floor by a chair, gets up on the chair and gets ready to jump on it. He counts One! Two! Three! and jumps, but before he does, Bob puts Mike's guitar on top of his and Mike smashes both of them.
6. They both pick up their guitars, try to put them together as good as possible, and then finish their song and leave.

This skit obviously is very slapstick and requires some tasteful deadpan acting by both guys. The results are hilarious. Damaged or second-hand guitars can be sometimes obtained free or very cheap from some merchants.

THE UGLIEST MONSTER IN THE WORLD

Bring in a guy with a blanket over his head who is the "monster." Tell everybody that this monster is so ugly that anyone who looks at him falls over dead. Three guys in the audience (clued-in) come up to try. They look under the blanket and sure-enough, they fall over deal. Now choose a girl (unsuspecting) to come up and look under the blanket, just to prove that girls are the stronger sex. She comes up, looks under the blanket, and when she does . . . the monster falls dead.

WILD WEST SHOW

This can be done one of two ways: either select seven kids to come to the front and take the parts below, or have the entire group get into seven smaller groups and each group takes one of the parts. Each part requires no acting, only sound effects. The person (or group) assigned to each part simply makes the appropriate sound effect each time their part's name comes up in the story, which is read by a narrator. The parts and the corresponding sound effects are:

1. The Cowboys ("Whooppee!")
2. The Indians (an Indian yell with war dance)
3. The Women (scream)
4. The Horses (clippety-clop with hands and feet)
5. The Stagecoach (make circular motions with arms, like wheels)
6. The Rifles ("Bang, bang!")
7. The Bows and Arrows ("Zip, zip," do the motions with hands)

The characters (or the groups) should try to over-do their parts and try to out-do each other. Every time one of the parts come up in the story, the narrator should pause and allow time for the sound effect or motion. Give the winner (whoever does the best job) a prize.

The Story:

It was in the days of **stagecoaches**, and **cowboys**, and **Indians**. Alkali Ike, Dippy Dick, and Pony Pete were three courageous **cowboys**. When the **stagecoach** left for Rainbow's End they were aboard, as were also two **women**, Salty Sal and a doll-faced blonde. The **stagecoach** was drawn by three handsome **horses** and it left Dead End exactly on time.

The most dangerous part of the journey was the pass known as Gory Gulch. As the **stagecoach** neared this spot, it could be noticed that the **women** were a bit nervous and the **cowboys** were alert, fingering their **rifles** as if to be ready for any emergency. Even the **horses** seemed to sense the danger.

Sure enough just as the **stagecoach** entered the Gulch there sounded the blood-curdling war cry of the **Indians**. Mounted on **horses** they came riding wildly toward the **stagecoach** aiming their **bows and arrows**. The **cowboys** took aim with their **rifles** and fired. The **women** screamed. The **horses** pranced nervously. The **Indians** shot their **bows and arrows**. The **cowboys** aimed their **rifles** again, this time shooting with more deadly effect. The leading brave fell and the **Indians** turned their **horses** and fled leaving their **bows and arrows** behind. The **women** fainted. The **cowboys** shot one more volley from their **rifles**, just for luck. The driver urged on the **horses** and the **stagecoach** sped down the trail.

YOU GOT ME BUDDY!

Scene: Two guys are sitting at a table in a restaurant, one reading a newspaper, so that you don't see his face. Another man dressed like a gangster enters the room and yells at the guy who is **not** reading the newspaper (from a distance).

Gangster: All right Butch, I got you at last! You been running from me too long and now I'm gonna finish you off!!!

Butch: Please, Big Al, I'll pay you back the dough I owe ya!

Gangster: Sorry, Butch, but you've had your last chance! (Shoots him several times with a blank gun.)

Butch: Ahhhhhhggg! You got me pal! You got me buddy! (Yelling) You got me pal!!!!

Gangster: Well, then, fall down and die already.

Butch: But you didn't get me . . . you got me PAL. (points to guy reading the newspaper and the guy reading the paper falls over dead.)

Publicity & Promotion

THE ACTION HANDOUT

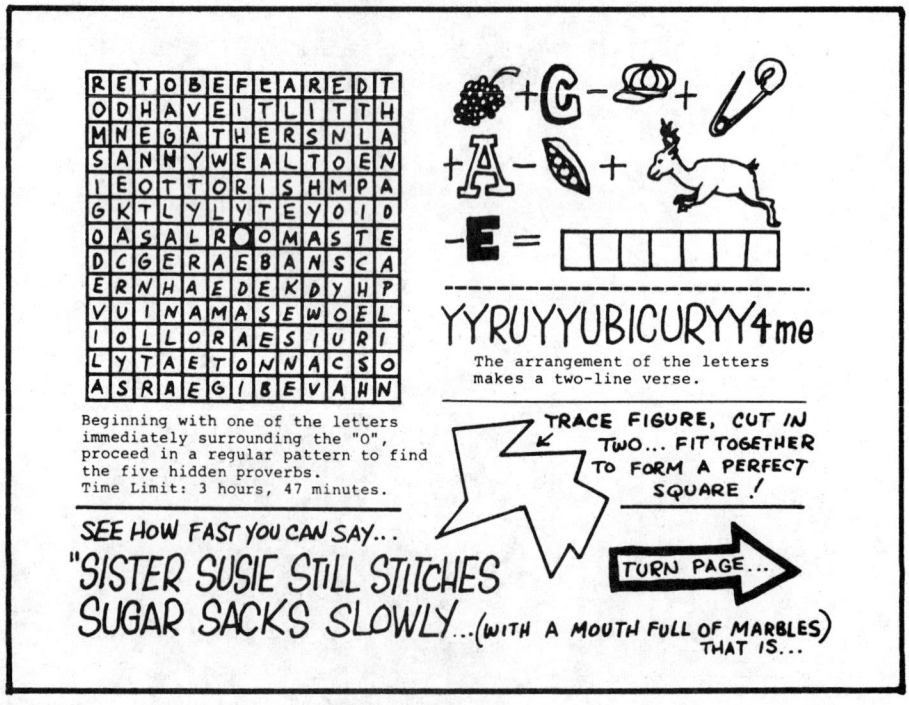

Next time you want to effectively advertise your youth meeting in a unique way, try this. Design a handout that folds in half, as illustrated above. The front can be anything you want, as long as it is attractive, and invites kids to open the handout and look inside. Inside the handout, print an assortment of puzzles, games, tongue twisters, and the like. On the back side of the handout, you can print all the details of your upcoming event. This handout is good because it not only gets your message across, but it gives the kids a bit of a challenge as well. For added fun, supply the "answers" to the puzzles at the meeting, and give a prize to anyone who could get them all correct.

"CONTEMPORARY CARD" HANDOUTS

One of the most effective ways to advertise a youth program or event is to print up a handout and have kids pass them out to their friends. It is more personal than using posters and less expensive than using the mail.

One type of handout that is always a winner is the type which not only informs, but also entertains. The handouts described here not only get the message across, but they also contain a joke or humorous story to lead the reader into the advertising. They are patterned after the contemporary greeting cards that are common in stationery stores, but they don't have to be nearly that large. The front of the card carries the "grabber" line, and when the card is opened, the "punch line" or joke is inside. The back side of the card can be used for the announcement.

The best way to produce these is to have someone draw the artwork for the joke and the advertisement, and then take it to a print shop that does "fast print" type printing. The cost for such printing is relatively low and the results are much better than using a mimeograph or ditto machine. A good size for this type of handout is 8½ by 5½ (half of a letter sized sheet) folded in half. That would make the front of the handout 5½ by 4¼ inches.

Front ("Grabber" line)    Inside (Punch Line) 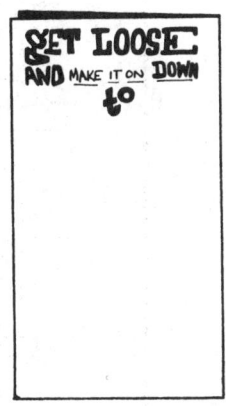   Back (Advertisement)

Following are a number of ideas for this type of handout. Included here is the complete joke, with the grabber line, the punch line, and a short "tie in" line that can be used to tie the joke in with whatever you are advertising. Use as much creativity as possible when designing your handouts and don't limit yourself to these. If you hear a good funny joke, it just might work out real good as a "contemporary card" handout.

	Grabber Line	Punch Line	Tie-In
1.	"I taught my pet fish to sing for you, but lately he's been singing off-key...."	And you know how hard it is to Tuna Fish	There's nothing fishy about...
2.	Latest clinical tests prove... 7 out of 10 Doctors...	Leaves 3.	Already proven...
3.	Choose your favorite nose: (Pictures of noses)	Now... if you're through pickin' your nose...	blow on over to
4.	Just so I wouldn't forget to tell you this, I tied my shoelace around my tongue.	Now I've got Athlete's Mouth.	Don't forget this....
5.	They say that success is 90% perspiration...	If that's so, you must be a tremendous success.	A program that's 100% successful
6.	The other day I saw a poor man who looked like he hadn't had a bite for weeks...	So I bit him.	Put the bite on your friends to come to...
7.	I bought you two authentic pearl buttons from the South Sea Isle of Bali.	Now you'll be the only guy in town with 2 pearl Bali buttons.	"Isle" meet you at...
8.	"Beautify Junkyards"	Throw something lovely away today.	A beautiful program.
9.	Stop! If you have any brains at all, you won't open this card!	Well, that settles that.	Brains or no brains, come to...
10.	Get Ready, Get Set,	Get Lost.	Get on down to...
11.	"Johnny, can you drive with one hand?" "Sure, baby!"	then wipe your nose, its running.	Drive on down to...
12.	Before you hang your clothes...	Make sure they get a fair trial	Hung up? Meet the gang at...

13. Always cross the street with the light.	that is, if you can rip it out of the pavement.	Rip on down
14. Here's a couple of real dillies:	"Dilly—Dilly"	A real dilly of a program:
15. "How to get Ahead"	(Picture of a guy chopping some guy's head off with an axe)	You'll laugh your head off at:
16. Note the Sad Story of the flea.	They all go to the dogs.	You can go to:
17. This morning I got up, shaved, showered, and splashed a little toilet water on my cheeks . . .	And then the lid fell and hit me on the back of the neck.	Fall in at . . .
18. "My girl is one of twins" "Really? How do you tell them apart?"	Her brother wears glasses.	An unmistakable program:
19. How do you get down off an elephant?	You don't, stupid, you get down off a duck!	Head on down to . . .
20. "Open in Case of Fire"	Not now stupid, In Case of FIRE!	A program that's really hot . . .
21. Hey, how come you are pulling that chain?	Man, did you ever try pushing one of these things?	Push your friends to be at . . .

THE FREE TICKET

Next time you plan a party, or special meeting in which you would like to draw a good crowd, print up a "free ticket," which is used in the same manner as a handout. Psychologically, the ticket has a lot more "drawing power" than a normal handout or announcement. Even though you do not charge anything to get in in the first place, people think they really have something valuable when they have a complimentary ticket.

Use the one below, if you wish, or design your own. Simply include all the details of your event in the empty space either vertically or horizontally.

For the best results, either have your information "typeset" by a company that does that sort of thing, or have an artist letter in the information in an attractive way.

COMPLIMENTARY TICKET
ADMIT ✱ ONE ✱

Put details of
your activity here

THE PEEP BOX

This simple idea is a great way to get kids to read bulletin board information. Build a big box out of plywood that is about three feet wide by three feet deep by three feet high. Mount it on legs and cut a hole in the bottom of the box just big enough for a kid to stick his head through. Paint the outside of the box or decorate it in some cre-

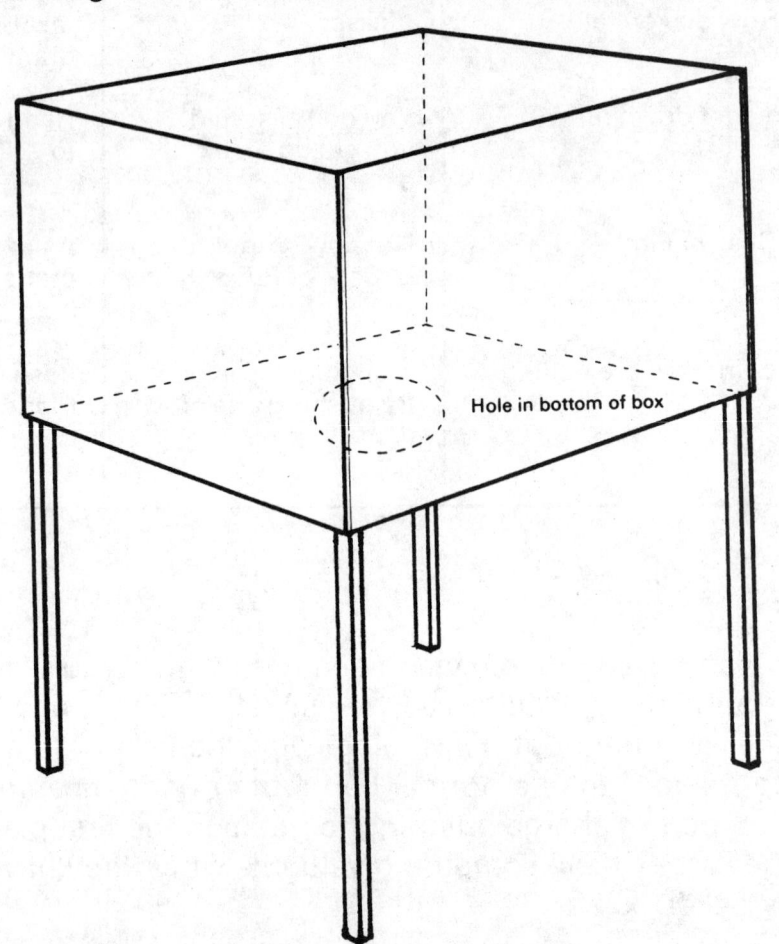

Hole in bottom of box

ative way. One side of the box should be hinged, so that it will open up and then be locked shut. A small light bulb of some kind inside the box (battery operated, perhaps) will light up the inside of the box. On the inside of the four walls of the box, hang your posters, announcements, pictures, and other items of interest. Kids now have to get under the box and poke their heads up through the hole in the bottom in order to see what is inside the box. If you are creative, and change the contents of the box every week, the kids will stand in line to see what is inside, just to satisfy their curiosity. Those same kids normally would ignore a traditional bulletin board.

For a variation of this, try putting a "blacklight" inside the box for illumination, and do all of your signs and announcements with fluorescent or "day-glo" markers or paints. The effect is fascinating. Also, a way to get good use out of your "peep box" would be to take it to a strategic location where there are a lot of kids who pass by, such as a popular youth hang out, or on a school campus itself, or just somewhere near the school where a lot of kids walk by on their way to school. It works great as a way to advertise coming youth events, as long as you make the box's contents as interesting as possible. (Contributed by Paul Sailhamer, Van Nuys, Calif.)

MAILERS

In spite of rising postage costs, the mail is still one of the best ways to announce coming activities and events to your young people. You should compile a good up-to-date list of names and addresses that you mail to regularly, and preferably you should have enough names on your mailing list to allow you to "bulk mail" to them, thus keeping your costs down.

The following letter ideas are only suggestions. The basic idea behind them is creativity. They are all different, unusual, humorous, and they are the kind of mail that a kid would look forward to receiving. As long as you are taking the time to prepare a letter of some kind, it may as well be a good one. It costs no more (usually) to be creative. The ideas presented here are some that have been used with success before, but you should try to create your own as much as possible.

Print your letters as neatly as possible. They should be easily read, and if possible, should not look "mimeographed." Not necessarily because of its "impersonal" feel, but simply because it looks ugly (usually). Use offset printing as much as possible. The "fast-print" companies that are common in most cities do one-color offset printing very inexpensively, and result in more of a professional look to your announcements. This is expecially true if you use transfer lettering (such as "Letraset" or "Formatt") or use artwork, cartoons, and the like.

With regards to lettering, clip-art, etc., you should check your local art stores to see what helps they have to offer along these lines. There are many sources of graphic aids that can give your advertising that "extra" touch. It is also suggested that you print letters such as the following examples on something other than "church letterhead." Usually colorful paper or your own personal letterhead brings better results.

Adapt these samples to fit your own needs, including your own information, names, dates, or whatever.

YOUTH GROUP I.Q. TEST

Match the column on the left with the one on the right:

1. Last Meeting
2. Lippo Residence
3. Sweaty Armpits
4. Monday, December 16
5. Goes "Ha-Ha-Ha-Clunk!"

a. Location for next Youth Group meeting.
b. before Christmas Holidays
c. a man laughing his head off.
d. Our Youth Director
e. Our next big party.

Score: 5 right—genius; 4 right—above average; 3 right—average; 2 right—slightly M.R.; 1 right—beyond help; 0 right—vegetable.

Regardless of your condition, there's a place for you at our next get-together, which will be held THIS MONDAY NIGHT at Lonnie Lippo's house, 4801 Vista Sombrero Dr., beginning promptly at 6:33 p.m. BE THERE!

Your friend,

If you thought our

LAST MEETING

was good, wait till you get a load of **this** one

Dear Student,

A routine check of school records has disclosed that you failed to complete kindergarten. We must, therefore, call to your attention Municipal Regulation 55-2938,11:

> "KINDERGARTEN MUST BE COMPLETED BY EVERY RESIDENT OF THIS COMMUNITY. THIS MANDATORY REQUIREMENT FOR A RESIDENTIAL PERMIT CANNOT BE WAIVED UNDER ANY CIRCUMSTANCES."

Your lack of kindergarten certification causes us to hereby order you to report for kindergarten registration on the first WEDNESDAY before the new term begins. In view of your advanced age, however, it will not be necessary for you to bring along your mommy.

Registration for the coming semester starts this **WEDNESDAY** night.

To whom it may concern:

The Traffic Ticket Accounting Bureau wishes to inform you that its records indicate an overpayment on your part for traffic tickets.

We cannot refund this overpayment, but you could do us a favor by hurriedly running up another traffic violation so that we may balance our books.

Therefore, we strongly urge you to speed on over to the next exciting meeting of . . .

WHAT GOES "HO-HO-HO-THUD!"?

Answer: It's Santa Claus laughing his head off.

"Yule" laugh your head off at the next exciting meeting of TEEN CLUB, next Wednesday night at 6:30. Don't miss it!

THE ALL PURPOSE LETTER
(Check the appropriate spaces—choose one)

Dear:
- ☐ Granny
- ☐ Fingers
- ☐ Elvin
- ☐ Swinger

Just wanted to tell you that I have been:
- ☐ watching my weight
- ☐ in love with my History teacher for the past two years
- ☐ picking my nose thinking of you
- ☐ washing my socks

After reading this letter, I hope you:
- ☐ still feel like calling me "Poopsie"
- ☐ get paroled soon
- ☐ brush your teeth
- ☐ fall out the nearest three-story window

Well, I have to close now because:
- ☐ I don't know any more 3-syllable words
- ☐ I need to study for my basket-weaving exam
- ☐ My mother is going to dress me
- ☐ My nose is bleeding

Signed:
- ☐ John Wayne
- ☐ Mama Bear, Papa Bear & Baby Bear
- ☐ Your Mother
- ☐ Charlie the Tuna

P.S. Youth Fellowship next Sunday night, 6:30 at the church.

CONGRATULATIONS!!!

You are one of the lucky winners in our exciting "WIN A BUCK" contest!

Your male Indian brave will be sent to you under separate cover. If, however, you do not receive your buck by next Tuesday night, then bring this card to the special "Winner's Meeting" at Kathy Hoaky's house, Tuesday night at 7 sharp.

SEX

Now that I have your attention . . . I'd like to remind you that next week, HI-LIFE will present a provocative program entitled:

"IS SEX A NO-NO?"

If you fit into one or more of the following categories, you need to come. (Check those that apply to you)

- ☐ You went to the drive in movie last weekend and you can't remember what movie you saw . . .
- ☐ You wish you had a club on your last date . . .
- ☐ Your boyfriend keeps taking you to see the "submarine races" at the river . . .
- ☐ Your boyfriend just bought a van with a bed in it . . .
- ☐ Your girlfriend likes to date in groups (like 50 or more) . . .
- ☐ Your boyfriend has an eight-track stereo, and a one-track mind . . .
- ☐ You believe in necking on the first date . . .
- ☐ You believe in necking *before* the first date . . .
- ☐ Holding hands turns you on . . .

Even if you don't fit into any of the above categories, you'll fit right in at HI-LIFE. The meeting starts at 7:23 p.m. sharp! See you there!

Your Youth Director

Campus Club social I.Q. TEST

Here is your personal copy of the CAMPUS CLUB SOCIAL INTELLIGENCE TEST. It will determine just how much fun you will be at a party, and will show you the areas in which you need to improve. Answer the following questions true or false:

True   False

☐   ☐   Kissing is when you grab another person's right hand with your right hand and shake it vigorously.

☐   ☐   The best way to be the "life of the party" is to stand against the wall, with one foot against the wallpaper,' looking cool.

☐   ☐   The most accepted way of getting another glass of punch is to dip your own cup into the punchbowl while joking, "Well, we all have the same germs, anyway . . ."

☐   ☐   The proper time to leave the party is at 3:00 in the morning, or when the hostess' father comes down the stairway with a shotgun, whichever comes first.

To check your answers, bring this test to the next meeting of CAMPUS CLUB, which just happens to be this Thursday night at 7. We may wind up having a party of our own! Don't miss it!

See you there!

THIS POSTCARD ENTITLES YOU TO ONE FREE NIGHT IN COUNTY JAIL.

(Tax and tip extra)

In order to receive this valuable free offer, merely follow the steps listed below:

1. Write down the important address below and keep it.
2. Crumple this card into a little ball.
3. Cram it down the throat of the nearest policeman.

This postcard is also good for one great evening at YOUTH FELLOW-SHIP in case you decide not to take advantage of the free offer above. Meet us at Bob Frit's house, 4040 Yucko Street, at exactly 7:13 p.m. See ya there.

YOU MAY HAVE ALREADY WON A VALUABLE PRIZE!!!

Here is your lucky number: 345678

If the lucky number above matches the winning number below, which was drawn at random (of course) then you may have won all or none of these exciting prizes:

1. An all-expense trip for two to Temecula. (One way)
2. An autographed picture of Elmer Floggy.
3. Three tickets to the Museum of Antique Lawn Mowers.
4. One pound of minced raccoon livers.

Here is the winning number: 345678

If your lucky number matches the winning number you may, or may not, have won the lovely prizes listed above. For further instructions, bring this card to our next "Hi-Life" meeting this Wednesday night, 7:00 at the church.

SILK-SCREEN PRINTING

or . . . "How to produce good-looking professional posters at a good-looking non-professional price."

ANYBODY can silk screen. That includes you. If you work with youth, need sharp publicity, but can't afford to pay your local printer or sign shop for high-quality posters, then we suggest that you read the following information very carefully.

The days of the "slopped-together" poster are over. No longer can you put up a poster that is a conglomeration of rubber cement, water paint, magazine clippings, and felt pens with a generous helping of glitter sprinkled around the edges, and expect it to be read, let alone get any response.

The silk-screen process of printing is a unique form of stencil printing that enables you to print on just about any surface in nearly any color, size, or quantity. Most billboards and posters that you see around town are silk-screened, as silk-screens range from simple hand operated home-made jobs (which we are going to explain on the following pages), to large motor-driven production screens. We are going to examine in a step-by-step manner, how to build your own silk-screen and how to operate it. The costs are surprisingly low, and the procedure is amazingly simple.

THE SILK-SCREEN ITSELF

A silk-screen consists of a wooden frame with silk attached and stretched to it, that hinges onto a flat piece of plywood (or table top) and may be purchased ready-made, or you can build one yourself, which is the most economical.

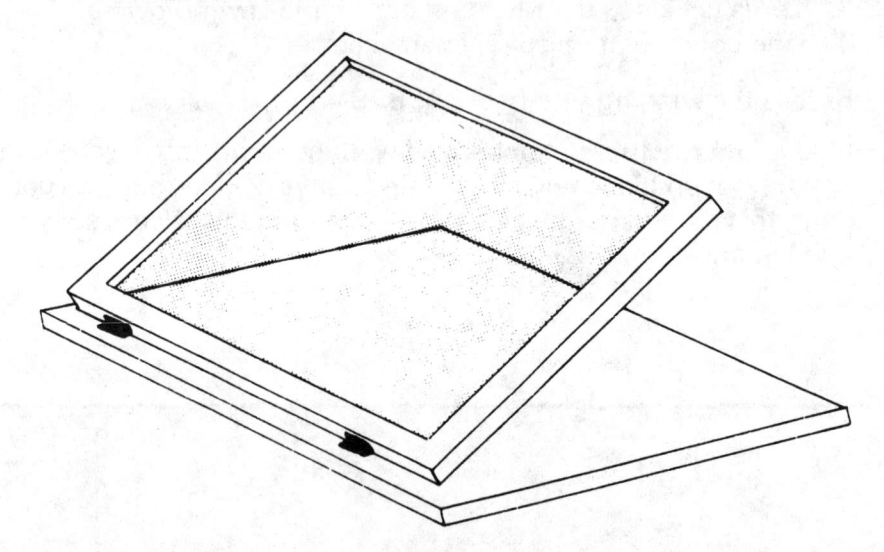

HOW TO BUILD A SILK SCREEN FRAME

The frame is simply four pieces of wood, fastened into a rectangular shape. The wooden pieces should be approximately 1½ by 1½ inches in size. It is best to miter the joints at a 45 degree angle, and nail with any nail of reasonable length. For added strength, use four metal "L" braces at the joints.

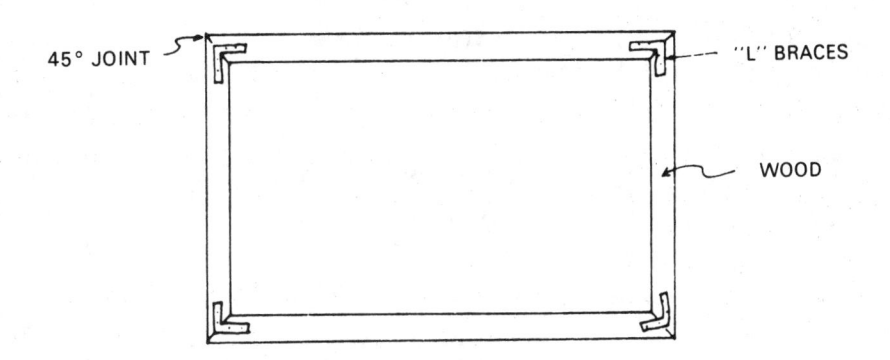

Decide what size posters that you will use the most. The inside dimentions of the frame should be at least 3 inches or so larger each way than the dimensions of the poster size.

THE SILK

You will need to buy silk (12xx pure screening silk) a little larger than your frame. It runs about $7.00 a yard, and comes a yard wide. Usually a half yard will cover most poster screens no larger than 18 inches wide. The silk is stretched tightly across the frame, and stapled. There are other methods of attaching the silk, but the stapling method is the simplest and easiest for the beginner. Start at one corner and work around, pulling the silk tight, and stapling at 1 inch spaces. Staple on an angle, and your stapling will do more good. For best results, wet the silk first with warm water, and leave wet while stretching, then dry later. After silk is attached, trim off excess silk.

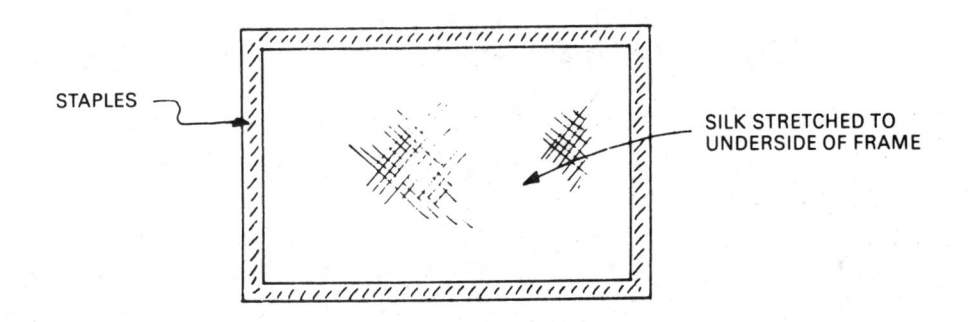

After it is stapled, smear some "Wilhold" or "Elmer's" glue (white) over the staples and let dry. This will prevent future tearing loose of the silk.

HINGE FRAME TO A FLAT SURFACE

Buy a small pair of hinges with removable pins. Also you will need a piece of plywood (1½ to ¾ inches wide will do), and hinge the frame to the plywood. Plywood dimensions should be a little larger than the outside dimensions of the frame.

THE STENCIL

Now you are ready to print some posters. You need a basic design for a poster first, which can be drawn with a pencil, or you can copy somebody else's poster, and adapt it to your own use. ANYBODY WHO CAN TRACE CAN MAKE A STENCIL.

To make a silk screen stencil, the basic pattern (your own poster idea) is "cut" out of a film called "Knife-cut Lacquer film," which can be purchased from a well-stocked art store or from a silk screen supply house. It consists of a shiny soft amber-colored film affixed to a dull plastic backing sheet.

Tape down your original design to a flat surface (desk top, etc.). You will need plenty of light. Work in a comfortable position. Cut a piece of lacquer stencil film just big enough to cover your design. Tape this film in position over the design, shiny side up.

Next, you will need an "X-acto" knife with a #11 blade. This can be bought in any art store.

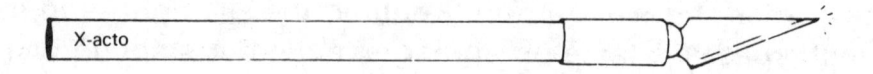

Keep the blade sharp. Dull blades only cause trouble.

Make a test cut. In a corner of the film, cut a small triangle. CUT THROUGH THE SHINY LACQUER FILM ONLY! DO NOT CUT THROUGH THE BACKING SHEET!

Insert the blade of your knife under the film in one corner of the triangle. Lift the film and strip away the triangle of lacquer film. (for practice)

Follow this procedure over your whole pattern—trace—cutting—stripping away the lacquer film, until you have removed film from all areas indicated on your pattern. The stripped or "open" areas will be those through which your ink will be impressed onto the printing surface. Remember, do not cut through or into that backing sheet. It is there to hold the stencil together. Always keep the film smooth and flat. Do not crease it.

FILM PEELED AWAY HERE. ONLY BACKING SHEET APPEARS.

LACQUER STENCIL FILM

ADHERING THE STENCIL TO THE SILK

Place the completed stencil between the silk (attached to the frame, of course), and the plywood surface, positioned in the center of the frame. It's a good idea to put the stencil on top of a few sheets of your stock (the paper you are printing on) to give the stencil a little added height. Then, lower the screen (frame and silk) onto the stencil. The stock under the stencil acts to bring the stencil sheet and silk into good contact. The stencil and silk must be in contact in all points in order to make a good adhere.

Now you are ready for the adhering process. You need two small, soft rags. Wet one rag with some "adhering solvent" or a good quality lacquer thinner. Either works fine, except that a special adhering solvent is usually more potent. The rag should be good and damp, but not dripping wet. With this rag, you rub (from the top side) the silk where the stencil shows through. Rub one area at a time, using firm strokes, and you will see the film actually "adhere." It sort of changes color. Immediately after using the wet rag, rub the same area with the dry rag to soak up any excess adhering liquid. Too much liquid "burns" or actually begins to dissolve the film. Follow each series of wetting strokes with drying strokes of the drying rag. Make sure the stencil adheres evenly all over. The stencil is now stuck-to, or "adhered" to the silk.

Let it dry for about 15 minutes. Then raise the screen and pull off the backing sheet. Pull down a corner of this backing sheet and carefully peel off slowly until the entire sheet is removed.

Caution: Always handle the adhering process in a warm, dry atmosphere.

SET THE REGISTER GUIDES

Put a piece of "stock" under the stencil (now adhered to the silk) and adjust to the position in which the pattern is centered, straight, etc. You will want to put some "register guides" or edge guides along two edges of the stock, so that all printing will print in the same place on every sheet. This is especially important for multi-colored printing.

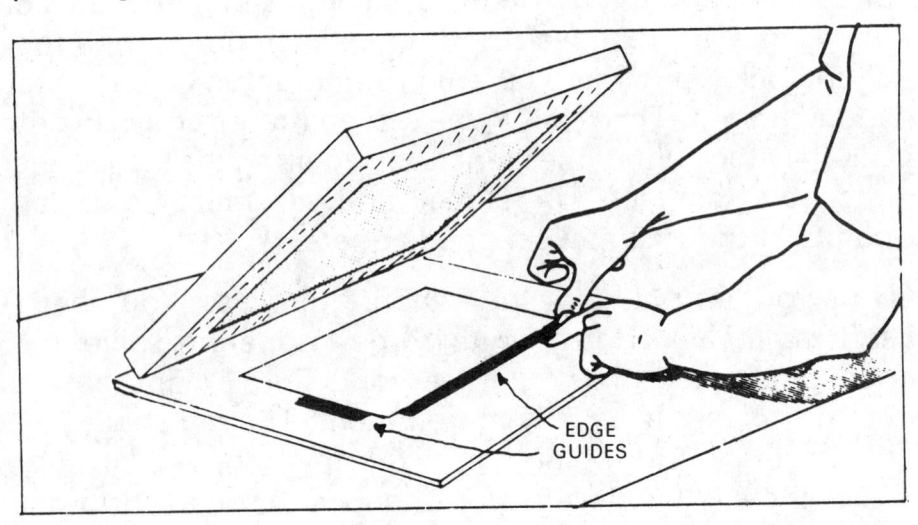

EDGE GUIDES

The edge guides can be made from pieces of thin cardboard, or pieces of making tape. Anything that will stay in place will work.

BLOCKOUT

Now you need to "block-out" all areas of the silk that are "open" around the edges of the stencil. This can be done many ways, but one good way is to cover the area on the underside of the silk with masking tape. When this is done you are ready to begin printing. The idea of blocking out is to leave only the image that you want printed open so that ink can pass through.

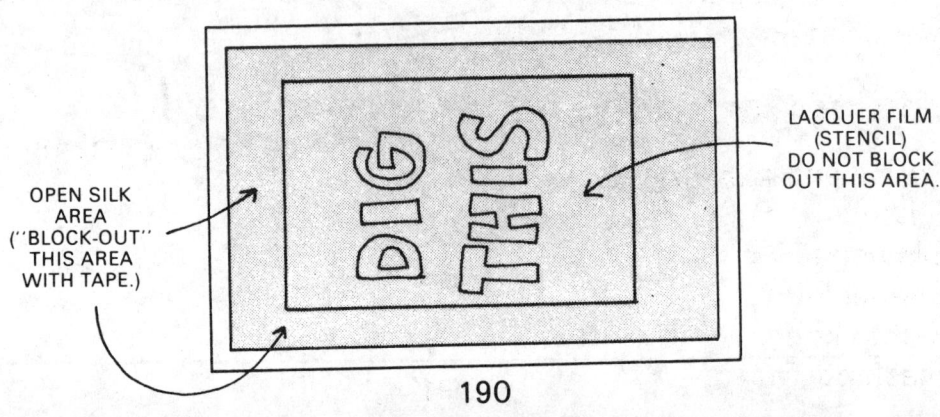

OPEN SILK AREA ("BLOCK-OUT" THIS AREA WITH TAPE.)

LACQUER FILM (STENCIL) DO NOT BLOCK OUT THIS AREA.

PRINTING

To print, you need to buy a "squeegee," which is a piece of wood with a strip of a specially treated rubber attached to it.

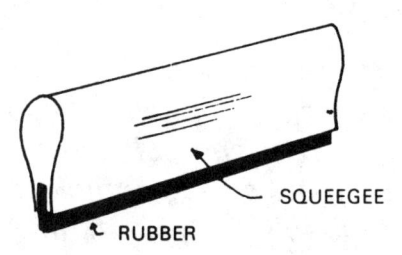

This, too, can be purchased at a good art store or a silk-screen supply house, and should be about ½ inch shorter than the smallest inside dimension of your frame.

Put one piece of paper in the edge guides. Lower the screen onto it. Pour some "silk-screen ink" (regular paint will not work) at one end of the screen on top of the silk. With the squeegee, you "pull" the ink firmly across the pattern, (once or twice at the most) and then lift the screen up. The paper will probably stick to the underside of the screen which is O.K. Pull it off and look at it . . .

YOU HAVE JUST SILK SCREENED!

Lay the printed stock somewhere to dry and keep going. You can print just as many as you want. If you are getting unwanted ink on your paper, chances are you need to block-out areas you missed with tape.

CLEAN UP

The screen must be cleaned after every operation. If you want to save the stencil and use it again, then you must leave it attached to the silk. Once you take it off it is gone. So, if you want to use it again, merely clean off all the masking tape, and wash the ink off with regular old paint thinner. (Do not use lacquer thinner) Use plenty of rags, and get the ink completely off. You can use the stencil over and over again. To take the stencil off, leaving the silk ready for the next stencil, simply soak it off with lacquer thinner (or adhering solvent which is more expensive). When the silk is clean, you can adhere a new stencil at any time in the future.

THINGS THAT YOU WILL PROBABLY NEED TO BUY:

Frame and plywood back
Silk
Squeegee
Stencil Film
X-acto knife
Masking Tape

Lacquer Thinner (or adhering solvent)
Paint Thinner
Silk Screen Ink
Paint Rags and a putty knife

> *Note: Most well-stocked art stores carry a line of silk screen supplies. Check the Yellow Pages of your phone book for a dealer, or call a sign shop and ask them where they get their supplies. For the complete set-up, which should keep you going for a while, it will probably run you about $15 to $20.*

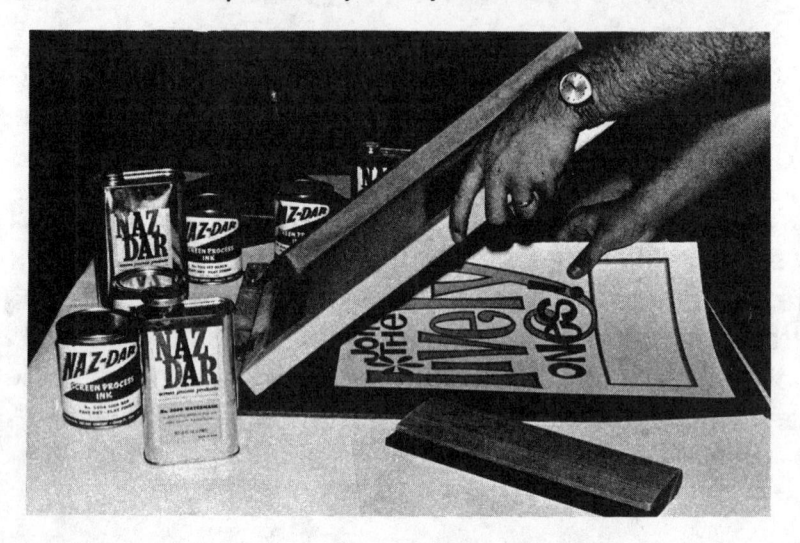